THE DILEMMA OF ISRAEL

HARRY B. ELLIS

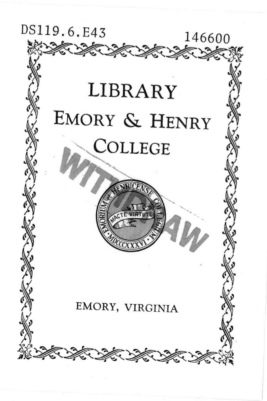
American Enterprise Institute for Public Policy Research
Washington, D.C. 20036

AMERICAN ENTERPRISE INSTITUTE
for Public Policy Research

Middle East Research Project

Professor George Lenczowski
University of California, Berkeley
Director

91st Congress
Second Session

ANALYSIS NO. 18

This Special Anaylsis is presented by the American Enterprise Institute as the fifth in its series within the framework of the Middle East Research Project. It was prepared prior to the death of President Nasser of the United Arab Republic.

Harry B. Ellis currently serves as *The Christian Science Monitor's* staff correspondent for Germany and Central Europe. He is a veteran foreign correspondent with that newspaper, having reported from over 30 countries in Europe, Africa, the Middle East, and Asia, and has published several books on Middle East affairs.

October 1970
Second Printing, January 1973

Library of Congress Catalog No. 70-134960

Price: $3.00

CONTENTS

I. DILEMMA

At this writing the prime minister of Israel is the same Golda Meir who, 20 years ago, slipped across the armistice lines to negotiate secretly with King Abdullah of Jordan. The 1948 War of Independence, or the first round of Arab-Jewish fighting, depending on the point of view, recently had ended. Already Abdullah had courted Arab disfavor by annexing unilaterally to his Hashemite kingdom those parts of Palestine (the West Bank) occupied by his Arab Legion. Now he compounded the difficulty by opening negotiations with the victorious Jews.

Abdullah's need was desperate. Swollen in size and population, his kingdom had lost its natural access to the Mediterranean Sea, when the British mandate gave way to the Jewish state. Only the inadequate port of Aqaba now connected Jordan with the water. Under military pressure, Abdullah had ceded to Israel a strip of territory about two miles wide along a 55-mile sector, slightly thickening the vulnerable waist of the Jewish state. The king now wanted a concession in return—access to Haifa for Jordan's trade.

The protracted talks ended in failure. Their existence was exposed both by Israel and by Abdullah al-Tell, a trusted Arab Legion colonel who deserted Abdullah, fled to Cairo, and denounced his monarch as a traitor. In every Arab capital a drumfire of condemnation descended on the king. On July 20, 1951, King Abdullah was shot dead by an Arab assassin as he entered Jerusalem's al-Aqsa mosque to pray.

With Abdullah that fateful morning was his 16-year-old grandson, the Amir Hussein. The following August 11, 1952 Hussein became King of Hashemite Jordan. Today, figuratively speaking, he looks out from his white palace in Amman, across the great divide of the Jordan River, to Jewish Jerusalem, whose leader is the woman with whom his grandfather negotiated two decades ago.

Hussein's predicament is vastly more complex than was Abdullah's. The latter's army, though unable to hold out longer against the Jews, at least had won parts of Palestine in battle. Included in its successes were Old Jerusalem, the crown jewel of Palestine, and some fertile areas of the West Bank. Abdullah did, however, lose access to the sea.

1

Hussein's Arab Legion, by contrast, lost all the West Bank, including Jerusalem, to the Israeli army in the blitzkrieg of 1967. What Hussein has left, the East Bank of Jordan, is a hot barren emptiness. Four-fifths of his remaining kingdom consists of desert. Never viable at best, Jordan today is even less so. Hussein must regain the West Bank, or his kingdom will remain perennially on dole, either to the United States or to oil-rich Arab sheiks.

But King Hussein's freedom of maneuver is meager. His country has become the host, willing or otherwise, involuntary in any case, of al-Fatah, the most aggressive Arab commando group. Yassir Arafat, chief spokesman of al-Fatah, rejects all political settlements with Israel and demands "liquidation of the occupying Zionist entity in Palestine." [1]

President Nasser of the United Arab Republic has expressed "complete support" of al-Fatah.[2] King Hussein, on whose territory al-Fatah bases itself, trains fedayeen (commandos), and launches attacks on Israel across the Jordan River, scarcely can do less. At best the king can try to restrain al-Fatah within certain uneasy bounds. When Arab guerrillas launched a rocket attack on the Israeli port of Eilat on April 8, 1969, drawing a retaliatory air raid on Jordan's hapless port of Aqaba, King Hussein temporarily arrested several al-Fatah commandos as a warning. This the king could manage. But for Hussein to open negotiations with Israel would be to invite assassination.

Israel's Situation Today

Israel's case is both better and worse than it was in 1949, when Mrs. Meir and other Jewish emissaries met with King Abdullah. For the first time since 1948 the state of Israel has secure frontiers. Syrian guns threatening kibbutzim north of the Sea of Galilee have been silenced and the Golan Heights cleared of Arabs. No longer is the Gaza Strip an Egyptian arrow thrusting into Israel. The Jordan River to the east and the Suez Canal in the west offer natural lines of defense. These are cease-fire lines, unsanctioned by international agreement. The U.N. Security Council resolution of November 22, 1967, called on Israeli forces to withdraw from all territory occupied during the six-day war. Pending a settlement, however, the fruits of victory give Israel a tactical advantage vis-à-vis the Arabs.

Israel paid for this security in 1967 by becoming the master of nearly one million Arabs. Must the Jewish state, to preserve its secure frontiers, accept these Arabs as citizens and become a bi-national state? If so, what becomes of the Zionist dream of a Jewish national home? Would not the higher Arab birth rate in time turn Israel into an Arab-dominated country?

At the beginning of 1968 Israel, excluding the occupied areas, had a population of 2,773,900 persons. Of this total, 2,383,900 were Jews and roughly 390,000 were Arabs. This included nearly 70,000 Arabs of Old Jerusalem, to whom Israel gave citizenship when it unified the Holy City. Israel's Druze Arabs—33,100 in number—are generally loyal to the Jewish state. Subtracting these Druze, Israel had within its borders almost 360,000 Arab citizens, whose loyalty was doubtful.

---

[1] Y. Harkabi, *Fedayeen Action and Arab Strategy* (London: The Institute for Strategic Studies, 1968), p. 31.
[2] John K. Cooley, *The Christian Science Monitor*, February 7, 1969.

2

The six-day war brought under Israeli control an additional 995,000 Arabs, including 599,000 on the West Bank. Another 356,000 lived in the Gaza Strip, 33,000 were in Northern Sinai, and 6,400 inhabited the Golan Heights.[3] Arab and Israeli statistics conflict. Israeli officials claim their postwar census showed 599,000 persons living on the West Bank. United Nations Relief and Works Agency's estimate, given to me by an American relief official just after the six-day war, was 900,000. This estimate was shared by the Jordanian government. No one can be sure just how many people fled to the East Bank during and after the June fighting. But whichever figure one accepts, Israel could not absorb so many Arab citizens without losing its character as a Jewish state.

Occupation an Alternative

The apparent alternative is for Israel to remain a colonial power, subjecting nearly one million Arabs to permanent military rule. Such a prospect is anathema to most Israelis. They are perfectly willing, even eager, to fight to defend the homeland. But they reject the concept of Jews reversing their historic role and becoming oppressors. On March 3, 1969, the U.N. Human Rights Commission, by a vote of 13 to 1, accused Israel of violating human rights in the occupied Arab territories. The 13 affirmative votes were cast mostly by Communist and non-aligned nations, while 16 Western-oriented powers abstained. Israel justly could call the vote one-sided. Nonetheless, the resolution touched Israel at a sore point.

The Jordanian city of Nablus on the West Bank illustrates Israel's difficulties in this regard. In June 1967, a few days after the guns fell silent, I visited Nablus and talked with the town's dignified Arab mayor. "In my town," this elderly man declared, "you will not find anyone, old or young, who does not want peace with our western neighbor." Outside Nablus, a few hours before, I had watched Arab boys and men climbing gingerly and awe-struck over the blackened ruins of Jordanian tanks, in which Arab Legionnaires had fought and died.

"Did that mean he was ready to cooperate with Israel?" I asked the mayor. He smiled. "Cooperation," he replied, "is the price of peace." At the time he spoke, the mayor and his townsmen still were shell-shocked by the fury of the war. Even then, however, the mayor—who subsequently resigned from office—had not been completely accurate in his assessment. His young Arab aide, who had greeted me courteously in the mayor's outer office, told me later with smoldering eyes that never would he cooperate with the hated Israelis, no matter what anyone else might do.

Apparently the resentment and anger expressed by that young man have gained dominance in Nablus. In April 1969, Israeli Defense Minister Moshe Dayan warned the Arabs of Nablus that, if they continued to "war" with Israel, their city would collapse "in chaos and destruction."[4] General Dayan's warning had been preceded by weeks of sporadic violence in Nablus, including strikes and rock-throwing demonstrations by Arab children.

(As a footnote, I recall the wondering admiration expressed by the young Israeli soldier to whom I gave a ride, at the beauty of the cut-stone houses of Nablus.

---

[3] Israeli government statistics.
[4] Associated Press report, Jerusalem, April 2, 1969.

These handsome homes, shaped by Arab craftsmen from the buff, yellow, and pink limestone of Palestinian cliffs, contrasted strikingly with the cement block architecture prevalent in Israel.)

A similar pattern of violence has emerged in Ramallah, Tulkarm, Old Jerusalem, and other West Bank centers, not to mention troubled Gaza. This kind of resistance, plus terrorist attacks by Arab commandos, can be put down by the Israeli army. But the process requires Jewish troops to institute reprisals, including the destruction of Arab homes, distracts Israelis from constructive work, and reinforces the image of Israel as an oppressor state.

Peace Agreement Needed

Only a peace agreement can pry Israel off the horns of its dilemma. But peace on what terms? The Security Council resolution of November 1967 required Israeli withdrawal from occupied areas, but spoke also of the right of each Middle Eastern state to "live in peace within secure and recognized boundaries." To the Arabs, this means restoration of the status quo ante, the surrender by Israel of all territory seized during the six-day war. This would certainly resolve Israel's binational/occupation dilemma, but at the sacrifice of safety.

"The majority of Israelis," declared Foreign Minister Abba Eban to the Paris newspaper *Le Figaro*, "desire the maximum security with the minimum of additional Arab population within the state of Israel." [5] "What we want," emphasized Prime Minister Golda Meir, "is not a guarantee of our security by others, but physical conditions and boundaries created in this country which will guarantee us. . . ." [6]

Defense Minister Moshe Dayan, the late Prime Minister Levi Eshkol, and other Israeli leaders have spoken in the same vein. Such statements indicate that the Israeli government has in mind certain territorial retentions, as part of whatever settlement may be reached. Israel is determined to hold onto the Golan Heights, already being settled by Jewish pioneers. Israelis do not claim that Syria's Golan Heights belong to Palestine. But they do insist that never again will Israeli villages in the exposed valley below become targets for Syrian guns.

Equally important to Israel is control of Sharm al-Sheik, the sandy fortress at the tip of the Sinai Peninsula. The Israeli government, under intense American and Soviet pressure, took its army out of Sinai after the 1956 Suez war, in return for the stationing at Sharm al-Sheik of a United Nations Emergency Force (UNEF). The presence of UNEF opened the Strait of Tiran and the port of Eilat to Israeli shipping. When President Nasser ordered the blue helmets out of Sinai in May 1967, Israelis—as their leaders had warned they would—took this as an act of war. Israel now intends to stay at Sharm al-Sheik and may insist on a Sinai land corridor to the isolated outpost.

A Labor party declaration published August 3, 1969, said that a district called "Merhav Schlomo," or Region of Solomon, would "be linked contiguously with Israel." Administratively, the Israeli army designates the entire southern region of

---

[5] From *Le Figaro*, as quoted by the *International Herald Tribune*, February 5, 1969.
[6] The *Times* (of London), March 27, 1969.

the Sinai Peninsula, including Biblical Mount Sinai, as Merhav Schlomo. This declaration, signed by Foreign Minister Abba Eban, Defense Minister Moshe Dayan, and Minister without Portfolio Israel Galili, appeared to indicate government policy.

Internationalization of Jerusalem's holy places, according to Mr. Eban, can be "envisaged." But Israelis are determined to retain political control of the unified city. For the first time since 63 B.C., when Pompey seized the city for imperial Rome, Jewish soldiers guard all the gates of Jerusalem, looking north to Damascus, west to Jaffa, and south to Bethlehem. To Israelis, rapt before the Wailing Wall, it is inconceivable that their city should be given up.

Gaza was an awkward economic and political problem for Egypt and is even more so for Israel, for the Strip's 356,000 Arabs, many of whom have been refugees for 20 years, are bitterly hostile to the Jewish state. Despite this, Israel prefers to keep the Gaza Strip, rather than allow Egyptian forces back. A cherished Israeli plan is to multiply vocational training opportunities for Gaza youth. Trained young people might find jobs elsewhere in the Arab world and even beyond. Canada and Australia, an Israeli official told me after the 1967 war, already had inquired about the availability of skilled Arab workers. Eventually, it is hoped, the Gaza Strip's population might be reduced to the point that the area's citrus groves and local industry could support it.

On the future of the West Bank and of the Sinai Peninsula, excluding Sharm al-Shiek and a connecting link of land, most Israelis remain relatively flexible. But retention of the Golan Heights, Old Jerusalem, Sharm al-Sheik, and the Gaza Strip is the premise from which Jewish leaders start their search for peace. Israel, in other words, chooses security over an easy resolution of its occupation dilemma.

Finally, Jewish leaders insist that Arabs and Israelis work out between them whatever solution may be achieved. A settlement imposed by the Big Four, Israelis believe, might be repudiated later by Arab governments, on the grounds they were coerced into it. Initial contacts would be allowed through intermediaries, including Gunnar Jarring, U.N. special representative in the Middle East. But in the end Israel wants Arab signatures on an arrangement discussed directly by Arabs and Jews.

"Why do the Arabs hate the Jews?" asked Moshe Dayan, speaking to American businessmen in Tel Aviv in January 1969. "Answer: They take us to be foreigners, invaders that took an Arab country and turned it into a Jewish state. And they are right about it. From their point of view, we did it. We didn't come here to contribute, or for a contribution to the Arab countries. We came here to establish our State because we feel that this is our homeland." [7]

A young Israeli, sipping coffee with me in an Arab café in Jaffa, put it another way. "I hate Germans," he declared, "because my family suffered from them. So I understand why Arabs feel about us as they do. They have suffered from us. But" —he shrugged his shoulders— "this is the end of the road for us Jews. We have no other place to go and, rightly or wrongly, here we stay."

---

[7] The *Sunday Times* (London), March 23, 1969.

5

Geography of Palestine

Palestine is bounded on the north by Lebanon, on the east by the Jordan rift, on the south by the Gulf of Aqaba, and on the west by the Sinai Peninsula and the Mediterranean Sea. Geographically, there is little about Palestine—an area roughly the size of Massachusetts—to inspire devotion.

The country begins in the south with the scorched Negev wilderness, at whose northern rim lies the Dead Sea. This fearsome lake, too saline to support life, the lowest spot on the earth's surface, is flanked east and west by desolate hills. Here were ancient Sodom and Gomorrah. Here, too, according to Scripture, Lot's wife, with her backward glance, became a pillar of salt.

North of the Dead Sea stretches the Jordan River valley, also largely barren, though dotted with green oases, of which Jericho is famous. West of the river rise the Judean heights, crowned by Jerusalem, and farther north, the hills of Samaria. On their western side these mountains slope down to a fertile coastal plain and to the Mediterranean Sea.

The heartland of the modern state of Israel is this long Mediterranean coastal plain, together with the grove-clad foothills of Judea and Samaria. Here lives the bulk of the nation's people, centered on Tel Aviv, Israel's largest city. Fifty-five miles north of Tel Aviv the coastal plain ends abruptly at Mount Carmel, where the city of Haifa, Israel's major port, looks down on the Haifa-Acre Bay. North of Haifa the hunched gray hills of Galilee extend to the border with Lebanon. In the Galilean hills dwell most of Israel's Arabs.

This, then, is Israel geographically—rugged Galilee in the north, a fertile coastal plain, a north-south chain of Samarian-Judean hills, parts of the Jordan valley, and, far to the south, the desert wilderness of Negev.

Political Frontiers Shift

Five times since World War I the political frontiers of Palestine have shifted, either in fact or on paper. Following the collapse of the Ottoman Turkish empire, the League of Nations assigned Britain a mandate over Palestine, including a large, mostly desert, tract east of the Jordan River. When Britain took up its Palestine mandate in 1920, there were 55,000 Jews in the country. An official census two years later showed 752,000 persons living in Palestine, of whom 650,000 were Arabs and 84,000 were Jews.[8]

The next change occurred in 1921, when Britain severed from its Palestine mandate those areas lying east of the Jordan River, named them the Amirate of Transjordan, and assigned them to an Arabian prince named Abdullah. In 1946 Britain gave political independence to Transjordan and Abdullah elevated his title to king.

A third frontier change took place on paper only. In 1947 an 11-nation United Nations Special Committee on Palestine (UNSCOP) recommended the partitition of Palestine into a Jewish state, an Arab state, and an internationalized Jerusalem. On November 29, 1947, this motion was adopted by the United Nations, with the

---

[8] *The Political History of Palestine Under British Administration* (New York: British Information Services).

6

United States, the Soviet Union, and France approving. By this time Jewish immigration had shifted the population ratio radically. At the end of 1946 Palestine contained 1,887,000 people, of whom 625,000 were Jews.[9]

Termination of the British mandate on May 14, 1948, Zionist proclamation of the state of Israel the same day, and the outbreak of the first Arab-Jewish war doomed the U.N. partition plan. When the shooting war ended on January 7, 1949, Israel had added 2,380 square miles, mostly in the Negev and western Galilee, plus a land corridor to Jerusalem, to the 5,670 square miles assigned to the Jewish state by the U.N. plan. Israel had increased its total area by more than 30 percent.

Egyptian forces held the Gaza Strip and King Abdullah, as we have seen, annexed to his kingdom those parts of Palestine west of the Jordan River, not occupied by Israel. These Middle Eastern frontiers—sanctioned only by armistice agreements—froze into permanence, with a brief interlude in 1956, when the Israeli army occupied Sinai.

During the 1948 war more than 700,000 Palestine Arabs fled from their homeland, 400,000 of them to Jordan. Many others ended up in the Gaza Strip, still others in Lebanon. This was the origin of the Palestine refugee problem. Today some of the children of those who fled in 1948 carry submachine guns for al-Fatah. Israel began its statehood with an estimated 879,000 persons, including 758,702 Jews and approximately 120,000 Arabs.[10]

From 1949 until June 1967 Israel had 590 miles of land boundaries, all with Arab neighbors. With Lebanon, Israel shared a 49-mile frontier. The Syrian-Israeli border was 47 miles long. With Jordan, Israel shared its longest boundary—329 miles. The frontier with Egypt in the Sinai Peninsula was 128 miles, plus 37 miles of border with the Egyptian-administered Gaza Strip.[11] To these frontiers the U.N. Security Council resolution of November 22, 1967, called upon Israel to return.

The latest—and to this point still existing—shift in Palestine's political borders resulted from the fighting in 1967. Only Lebanon among Israel's neighbors was unaffected territorially by the six-day war. Israeli forces seized the Golan Heights from Syria, pushed the Hashemite Kingdom of Jordan east of the Jordan River, and cleared the Egyptians from Gaza and Sinai.

The old armistice lines, which had come to be accepted by the world—though not by the Arabs—as definitive, now were replaced by cease-fire lines, a terminology more fragile than armistice. For Israel itself, and equally for Egypt and Jordan, the difference between the armistice lines of 1949 and the cease-fire lines of 1967 has profound meaning for the future.

[9] *Ibid.*, p. 32.
[10] Israeli government figures.
[11] Israeli government figures.

II. IN THE BEGINNING

The conflict between Arabs and Israelis is rooted in the devotion of two Semitic peoples to a single land. To the ancient Hebrews, Palestine was the anvil on which their sense of nationhood was hammered out. Abraham, the "friend of God," received a promise from the Lord God: "And I will give unto thee, and to thy seed after thee, the land wherein thou art a stranger, all the land of Canaan, for an everlasting possession" (Genesis 17:8). This covenant was the foundation of Jewish attachment to Palestine.

Centuries of historic and religious development, from Abraham through Moses to David, constituted a unique marriage of land and people, celebrated in the consummate literature of the Old Testament. Then came the conquest of Palestine by Assyria and Babylon, from the eighth to the sixth centuries B.C. This inaugurated the Diaspora, or the worldwide scattering of the Jews. The hearts of the exiles turned ever back to the Promised Land. To religious Jews down through the ages, and later to political Zionists, the Diaspora simply interrupted a God-ordained communion between Palestine and Jews.

The Arab connection with Palestine began centuries after the Jews had been thrust out. In the seventh century A.D. desert tribes, impelled by Mohammed's new religion, boiled up from the Arabian Desert and conquered Jerusalem in 638 and Caesarea in 640. Palestine became a small, though significant, segment of an Arab empire which spread, within a century of the Prophet's death, from the frontiers of China to the Atlantic coasts of North Africa and Spain.

Palestine's special quality to the Arabs related to Islam. Moslem doctrine held that Mohammed had been transported miraculously to Jerusalem, prior to his ascent to the seventh heaven. Later the magnificent Dome of the Rock complex, including the al-Aqsa Mosque, was built to commemorate the Prophet's pilgrimage. Jerusalem, after Mecca and Medina in Arabia proper, became the third most holy city in Islam.

From the time of the Arab conquest until today, Arabs have lived consecutively in Palestine. The country was conquered by the Turks and later administered by

Britain under mandate. But there was no widespread dispersion of the indigenous Arabs. This occurred only after the 1948 war between Arabs and Jews.

Both peoples share a common origin as Semitic nomads and both cherish hallowed traditions, bound up with Palestine. To some extent these traditions are mutually exclusive, or have come to seem so, during the crucible years since World War II.

Zionism is Born

.Late in the nineteenth century the dream of exiled Jews, "next year in Jerusalem," took on political content with the birth of Zionism. This movement, named after Mount Zion in Jerusalem—symbolic center of Jewish national life—embraced both religious and secular Jews.

To Zionists, the Jews of the Dispersion were a people of the ghetto. This ghetto, or sense of separation, was both physical and mental. In Eastern Europe particularly, Jews long had been confined to places of physical separation, of walled exclusion from gentile life, in cities and towns.

Hitler was not the first anti-Semite to force Jews to wear a distinctive badge. The Fourth Lateran Council of the Roman Catholic Church, meeting in Rome in 1215, required the Jews of Europe to wear a yellow patch on their clothing to distinguish them from gentiles. Henry II, ruler of Castile in the late fourteenth century, issued a similar order for the Jews of his kingdom.

In 1492, the year made famous by Columbus, 300,000 Jews were expelled from Spain by Ferdinand and Isabella. Earlier, the Jews of France and in parts of Germany had suffered a similar fate. In 1096 Christian Crusaders had begun their work against infidels by killing more than 10,000 Jews in cities along the Rhine.[1]

This pattern of expulsion, ghetto confinement, and pogrom prevailed throughout much of Europe in the Middle Ages. A notable exception was Holland, which, after the Protestant Reformation, provided a place of haven for Jews. Along with persecution went the forced exclusion of Jews from land ownership, the practice of agriculture, and membership in the craft guilds. Many European Jews, either because they were required to do, or because they were cut off from primary pursuits, perforce became moneychangers. Hitler and other anti-Semites later condemned the Jews for developing a skill which, in part, gentile edict had forced them to acquire.

By the late nineteenth century emancipatory forces unlocked by the French Revolution had improved the lot of Jews in western and central Europe. Eventually France, Prussia, Austria, Italy, and other nations gave citizenship rights to Jews. Countless Jewish families in these countries assimilated—gave up their concept of Jewish separation. Even those who clung to the religion of their fathers regarded themselves as Frenchmen or Germans, not as Jews in an alien land.

Persecution in Eastern Europe

The position of Jews in Poland deserves a special word, for the prevailing anti-Semitism of Communist Poland is not rooted in the country's history. Indeed,

---

[1] Rufus Learsi, *Israel: A History of the Jewish People* (Cleveland: The World Publishing Co., 1949), p. 273.

10

during the persecution of Jews in western Europe in the Middle Ages, many uprooted Jews found a congenial home in Poland. They were protected by royal charters granting them cultural and religious autonomy and a measure of local self-government. A law passed by the Polish parliament forbidding nobles to engage in commerce enabled the Jews to attain a dominant position in Polish commercial life, particularly in the important grain trade. Before the Partitions of the Polish-Lithuanian Commonwealth in the late eighteenth century, the Jewish community in Poland became the largest single center of Jewish life in Europe.

This situation changed following the partitions of 1772, 1793, and 1795, when Poland's territory was divided among Prussia, Austria, and Russia. Most of Poland's Jews now found themselves under Russian control. Here the pattern of anti-Semitism was consistent. As early as the seventeenth century Cossacks had laid waste an estimated 700 Jewish communities in Poland.[2]

Progressively the czars squeezed the Jews into a restricted territory, called the Pale of Settlement, in the Ukraine and adjacent western areas of Czarist Russia. This Pale, though it embraced thousands of square miles of land, was an extended form of ghetto. Various kinds of discrimination followed, including the drafting of Jewish boys for 25 years of military service, in the hope of weaning them away from family and Judaism.

The year 1881 brought a culmination. Royalists charged the Jews with complicity in the assassination of Czar Alexander II. Russian mobs officially were allowed to sack Hebrew communities. In 1887 the czarist government sharply limited the number of Jewish students allowed to attend high schools and universities. Under the impulsion of successive pogroms, Jews began to flow out of Russia. Between 1881 and 1914, an estimated two million Jews left Russia for the United States alone.

This development coincided with the rise, within Poland proper, of a Polish middle class. For the first time in Polish history Poles began to compete with Jews in commerce, industry, and the professions. Poland after World War I regained the Western Ukraine and acquired many Jews as well, fleeing now-Communist Russia. The problem of absorbing these alien Jews, many of whom could not speak Polish, plus the rise of nationalism and a middle class in Poland, competing with Jews on their traditional ground, inevitably caused tensions. Nonetheless, Jews continued to play a leading and accepted role in many spheres of Polish life during the 1930s, when German Jews already were falling beneath Hitler's shadow.

To many Russian Jews in the late nineteenth century, emigration to the New World—or, later, to Poland—provided no answer. They looked about Europe and saw in dispersed Jewry a rootless people. Many Jews, living physically separate, had withdrawn into a mental ghetto, concentrating on the minutiae of Judaic religious law. Others who, through talent and opportunity, had broken out of the ghetto, strove to immerse themselves in the mainstream of gentile life—socially, culturally, economically, and in many cases religiously, through conversion to Christianity.

Both methods of escape were opposed by Zionists. They held that the only true release from anti-Semitism and a minority status lay in a return to Palestine, the

---

[2] See Learsi, *op. cit.,* for a history of European Jewry.

11

Promised Land. The Diaspora, the Zionists argued, had exaggerated those aspects of Jewish life which were peculiar and separate. This in turn had deepened gentile aversion and exposed the Jew to perennial oppression.

All this, according to Zionists, would be changed through a return to Palestine. Striking down roots into the land of their fathers, farming their own soil, the Jews of Palestine would create a genuine Jewish environment, including a broad-based economy and a rich indigenous culture. Finally, political statehood would restore national identity to the Jews.

Zionists Organize

In 1884 the Choveve Zion (Lovers of Zion) met in the Russian city of Pinsk, to formulate their ideas on the Jewish return to Palestine. Thirteen years later Theodor Herzl, an Austrian Jewish journalist whose book, *The Jewish State*, had been published in 1896, convened the First Zionist Congress in Basel, Switzerland. Members of the Choveve Zion were Russian Jews, centered in Pinsk. Herzl was a Westerner, who at first had little or no knowledge of the striving of the Pinsk Jews. Yet they shared a basic longing for a Jewish national home in Palestine.

Leadership of the Zionist movement devolved on Herzl until his death in 1904. Annual, and later biennial, Congresses became the legislative and debating forum of the World Zionist Organization. A Zionist bank was created under the name Jewish Colonial Trust. In 1900 the Fourth Zionist Congress, held in London, established the Jewish National Fund, whose function was to purchase land in Palestine. This land would be leased to Jewish settlers, but title would be held by the Fund in perpetuity in the name of the Jewish people.[3]

In Western Europe, Zionism ran head-on into the opposition of assimilated Jews, especially the wealthy. Such Jews, even those who had retained Judaism as a faith, regarded themselves as nationals of the countries in which they lived. They held that Zionism, by emphasizing the apartheid of the Jewish people, tended to arouse the very anti-Semitic passions which Zionists yearned to avoid.

Zionist leaders, speaking primarily from the background of Eastern European experience, rejected this view. They claimed that, whenever Jews reached a certain point in numbers and influence within a gentile society, Christians would turn against them. Chaim Weizmann recalled a conversation he had had on the subject with an assimilated German Jew. The latter argued that anti-Semitism would end only when the Germans became aware of the good qualities of Jews. "Herr Doktor," burst out Weizmann, "if a man has a piece of something in his eye, he doesn't want to know whether it's a piece of mud or a piece of gold. He just wants to get it out!" [4]

Relationship Between Zionism and Judaism

Persecution of the Jews by the Nazis made meaningless this split between Zionists and assimilationists. The overriding need, on which all Jews could unite, was

---

[3] A detailed study of Zionism is provided by Chaim Weizmann's *Trial and Error* (New York: Harper & Brothers, 1949). This is the autobiography of the man who became the first president of Israel.

[4] Weizmann, *op. cit.,* p. 32.

to save European Jewry from extinction. With the passage of years since the Nazi holocaust, and with Israel established as a sovereign state, the old debates arise. What is the relationship between Zionism, the political movement which led the fight to create Israel, and Judaism, the religion which had its birth in ancient Palestine? How should an American or British or French Jew regard Israel? Can such a Jew be a loyal citizen of his motherland and at the same time a Zionist supporter of the Jewish state?

Basic to the Jewish religion is the concept that the Jews are a chosen people, through whom God works out purposes invisible to man. The ultimate goals of the Deity are neither to be swayed nor anticipated by human endeavor. Thus there are Jews within the state of Israel—principally members of Agudat Israel, an ultra-Orthodox religious group—who hold that the creation of a Jewish political state interfered in the divine processes of God. A tiny sect called Naturei Karta carries this conviction to the point of not recognizing Israel as a state.

Orthodoxy of this type had begun to be undermined in Europe, before Zionism was founded. Moses Mendelssohn foreshadowed Reform Judaism in the nineteenth century, when he translated the Pentateuch into German and modernized liturgical practice. Reform Judaists built on the pioneer work of Mendelssohn and rejected the doctrine that the Jews of the Dispersion were in exile, from which they would be redeemed through the restoration of Palestine. Ultra-Orthodox and Reform Jews, different as day and night in spiritual witness, share an aversion to the political nationalism of Zionism.

Mendelssohn also foreshadowed Zionism, by beginning to interpret Jewish history in terms of nationalism.[5] Moses Hess, a German Jewish socialist who died in 1875, is described by Alan R. Taylor as the "first systematic Zionist thinker."[6] Hess saw the Jews as one among many national types, destined eventually to exist in harmonious relationship with each other. This thrust upon Jews the duty to preserve the Jewish character, to elucidate Jewish nationalism, and to bring an end to centuries of exile through a return to Palestine.[7]

In Russia, meanwhile, Jewish intellectuals influenced by populism and socialism developed their own theories of Jewish nationalism, particularly after the onslaught of official Russian anti-Semitism in 1881. The ideology of this movement, named haskalah (enlightenment), called for the revival of the Jewish nation—a national rather than religious entity—in its own land.

Mendelssohn, Hess, and other Germanic thinkers paved the way for the Zionism of Herzl. The eastern haskalah, together with other schools of Jewish philosophy in Russia, flowered into Choveve Zion, focused on the city of Pinsk. It fell to Herzl to combine these forces of western and eastern Zionism around the common theme of Palestine.

Zionist ranks include religious Jews. Primarily, however, Zionists interpret Jewish history in secular terms. Object of the movement was not to restore a religious center in Jerusalem, except as a by-product, but to reconstitute the nation of

---

[5] See Alan R. Taylor, "Zionist Ideology: An Interpretive Analysis," *The Middle East Journal,* Autumn 1964.

[6] *Ibid.,* p. 432.

[7] Moses Hess, *Rome and Jerusalem, a Study in Jewish Nationalism* (New York: Black, 1918, translated by Meyer Waxman).

Israel within its Promised Land. Many early Zionists were political activists and atheists, not identified with a religious sect.

Assimilated Jews by definition reject Zionism. They accept, as part of their loyalty to their various homelands, the same rights and duties which devolve on gentile citizens. Non-Zionist Jews leave the choice of loyalty up to each Jew. But they deplore the Zionist effort to lump together all Jews, regardless of domicile, into a single nation, part of which has been ingathered in Israel.

American Zionists find themselves in a curious conflict with leading Zionists in Israel, who contend that every Jew calling himself a Zionist should settle in Israel. This strife broke into the open in 1951, when David Ben-Gurion asserted that every Zionist "must himself come to Israel as an immigrant."[8] Ben-Gurion amplified this in 1957, declaring that the Jew "who buys a shekel (i.e., helps Israel with money) and assimilates in practice" could not be considered a Zionist.[9] This challenged countless American Zionists, whose generosity had done much to aid Israel economically and whose political influence in Washington had helped to shape American policy toward the Jewish state. American Jewish leader Nahum Goldmann replied that, "since the ingathering of exiles to Israel might consume centuries, Zionism also had the duty to support Jewish life in the Diaspora."[10]

Broadly speaking, American Jewry is split two ways on the subject of Zionism. Non-Zionists deplore the concept of dual loyalty implied by Zionism. Many such Jews reject even the term assimilationist, on the grounds that it suggests a difference between them and other American citizens. American Zionists affirm their political loyalty to the United States, but see no conflict between this and giving financial and lobbying support to Israel.

Waves of Immigration

The First Aliya, or wave of immigration of dispersed Jews back to Palestine, took place from 1882 to 1904, without organized Zionist support. Though inspired by sentiments of Choveve Zion, these early settlers depended upon the philanthropy of Baron Edmond de Rothschild to establish them in Palestine. Their customary effort was to found small business enterprises, in which labor was provided by Arabs and management by Jews.

The Second Aliya, from 1904 to 1914, derived its support from the World Zionist Organization, through the Jewish Colonial Trust and the Jewish National Fund. The typical unit of settlement during this period was the kibbutz, or collective, conceived by Zionists as the ideal social organization, through which Jewish pioneers would wrest a living from the harsh soil of the Promised Land.

To understand the essence of kibbutz life, one must place it against the background of a dispossessed people seeking to establish a homeland. The kibbutz was designed to lay the groundwork for a flourishing Jewish economy, capable of sustaining the anticipated immigrants. The kibbutz had, therefore, to embody a love of work, an attraction to the soil, and an unquestioned devotion to the larger com-

---

[8] *Jerusalem Post,* August 17, 1951.
[9] "Proceedings of the Jerusalem Ideological Conference," p. 149, as reported by Taylor, *op. cit.,* p. 442.
[10] *Ibid.*

munity. Zionists drew their inspiration from a number of sources, including the European scouting movement, German Wandervögel youth groups, and from the religion of labor developed by Aaron David Gordon, an early Russian Zionist. The kibbutz in Palestine also has been called the first implementation of Socialist theories of collectivism, as advanced by Russian Socialists.

"How shall this nation," wrote Gordon, "throw off two thousand years of the Diaspora? We, an alienated people with no roots in the soil and who are thus deprived of the power of creativeness, a people who have lived as parasites in towns and to whom by force of circumstances this has become second nature, we must return to the soil, to independence, to nature, to a regenerated life of work." [11]

All property within the kibbutz was to be collectively owned and parceled out to members according to need. Work would be assigned to each member on a rotating basis, through a committee representing the community as a whole. All details of living, including the rearing of. children, were to be collectively organized. Members adept at teaching and nursing would staff the nurseries, where children of the kibbutz would eat, play, study, and sleep. Each day a quiet hour, usually before the evening meal, was to be set aside for parents and children to visit together. All needs of each chaver (member) were to be met by the community, in sickness and health. Children of talent were to be sent abroad at kibbutz expense to continue their education.

A system so demanding of human nature, with its denial of parental care and of the private property instinct, is best adapted to pioneer conditions. Over the years the more radical features of kibbutz life have been relaxed. A husband and wife, though they still live apart from their children, are allowed to acquire some things of their own—a radio or television set, a small refrigerator for evening snacks, decorative articles expressing personal taste. The traditional single rooms have expanded into small apartments, where kibbutz resources permit. No longer must a woman turn in her clothes to the laundry and pick up another set, which may or may not fit and please her.

Degania, the first kibbutz, was founded in 1909, near the Sea of Galilee. Aaron David Gordon, though never a member of Degania, helped to shape the community's life and himself worked in Degania's fields. "At Degania," wrote Joseph Baratz, "many of us planted more trees than Gordon but nobody planted them so neatly, so beautifully. Everything he did was like this, whether it was sweeping a room or making a bed, or writing, or arranging the table at which he wrote (he wrote in the early hours of the morning before joining us in the fields at sunrise). So a man works when he works not for duty but for love, and respects the things he uses." [12]

Today, according to the Israeli government, there are 233 kibbutzim, with populations ranging from 60 to 2,000. Some kibbutzim have become bustling manufacturing centers, though still collectively owned. Kibbutz Yagur, near Haifa, is known for its machinery, including parts for tractors and other farm vehicles.

---

[11] Joseph Baratz, *A Village by the Jordan* (New York: Roy Publishers, 1955), p. 83.
[12] *Ibid*, p. 80.

15

Fruits and juices put up by kibbutz Gan Shmuel grace grocery shelves from Bucharest to Cologne.

In recent years the kibbutz movement in Israel has about held its own. Roughly as many people leave kibbutzim as join them. Israel today is an established entity and kibbutz zeal flourished when a state remained to be consolidated and raw land to be conquered. A flurry of new kibbutz activity has taken place in the Golan Heights of Syria, since the 1967 war. Several collectives have been established on the hills by Nahal, pioneer organization of the Israeli army, aided by veteran chaverim from older kibbutzim.[13]

By 1914, when the Second Aliya ended, about 50 Jewish agricultural settlements existed in Palestine, farming 100,000 acres of land. Tel Aviv, at first a suburb of Arab Jaffa, had become an all-Jewish city. Funds raised by the World Zionist Organization were being disbursed in Palestine by a Palestine Department directed by Arthur Ruppin. The next wave of immigration, called the Third Aliya, was dated 1919-24. From that time on the tide of immigration swelled so rapidly that it was reckoned in years, rather than Aliyas. The next task was to supplement settlement on the land by founding a political state in Palestine.

[13] Melford E. Spiro, *Kibbutz, Venture in Utopia* (Cambridge: Harvard University Press, 1956), describes the origin and development of the kibbutz movement.

III. ISRAEL'S DIPLOMATIC HISTORY

In 1903 Theodor Herzl electrified the Sixth Zionist Congress, meeting in Basel, by disclosing a British government offer to give the Jews an autonomous territory in Uganda, in British East Africa. Herzl stressed to his fellow Zionists that Uganda, while not a substitute for Palestine, offered an immediate solution to the crisis of Eastern European Jews, then suffering from Czarist pogroms. He cast Uganda in the role of a large-scale relief operation, with eventual settlement in Palestine to be held in abeyance. Background to Herzl's advocacy of Uganda were his unsuccessful efforts to persuade the Ottoman Turkish government, then in control of Palestine, to allow formation of a charter company to promote Jewish settlement in the Holy Land.

First reaction of Zionist delegates was elation that a Great Power for the first time had made a concrete offer of statehood to the Jewish people. But elation soon gave way to overwhelming opposition from Russian Zionists—the very people whom Westerners had envisaged as the chief beneficiaries of Uganda. The leaders of Eastern Jewry taxed Uganda supporters with having lost touch with the age-old longing of the Jewish people for Palestine. Zionism, in the Russian view, existed only for the purpose of working toward a Jewish national home in the Promised Land.

Final rejection of the British offer of Uganda came in 1905, at the Seventh Zionist Congress. Herzl by now was dead and leadership of the Zionist movement was passing to the Russian wing, with Chaim Weizmann as its leader.

Earlier, Herzl and other Zionists tentatively had discussed with British officials the possibility of Jewish settlement in El Arish, a sandy strip of coastline between Palestine and Egypt, including the Gaza Strip. The conferees decided that lack of water in Sinai precluded colonization of El Arish. (Following the 1967 war, when Israeli scientists were free to explore occupied Sinai, geologists reported finding vast reserves of water underlying the Sinai wilderness. If tapped, the geologists concluded, Sinai might be transformed into an area capable of supporting large numbers of Arab refugees now crowded into the oases of Gaza.)[1]

---

[1] David Spanier, the *Times* (of London), April 7, 1969.

17

Disgruntled supporters of Uganda broke away from the main Zionist body to found the Jewish Territorial Organization. This faction, which existed until 1918, sought in vain for some alternative to Palestine for Jewish settlement. The disaffection of this group cleared the way for the world Zionist movement, now led by Eastern Jews, to press for a Palestine solution.

Britain and the Balfour Declaration

From a background of British citizenship, which he had acquired, and through his services as a chemist to the British war effort, Weizmann was ideally placed to urge the Zionist cause on British leaders. Early supporters of Zionism in Britain included Lloyd George, then Chancellor of the Exchequer, Winston Churchill, Arthur James Balfour, First Lord of the Admiralty and later Foreign Secretary, and C. P. Scott, editor of the *Manchester Guardian.*

The Zionists foresaw as logical and desirable a British mandate over Palestine after the war, when the Ottoman Empire had collapsed. British control of Palestine would afford the Jews a friendly climate in which to establish themselves on the land. In return, Zionists could promise the British government a pro-British bastion in the Middle East, when the Zionist state had been created. This latter possibility appealed to British strategists, responsible for the security of India.

As the war drew to a close, British officials sought from Weizmann a clear statement of the Zionist position in relation to Britain and Palestine. On July 18, 1917, the Political Committee of the Zionist Organization presented the following formula, to be considered by the British Cabinet:

> His Majesty's Government, after considering the aims of the Zionist Organization, accept the principle of recognizing Palestine as the National Home of the Jewish people and the right of the Jewish people to build up its national life in Palestine under a protection to be established at the conclusion of peace, following upon the successful issue of the war.
>
> His Majesty's Government regard as essential for the realization of this principle the grant of internal autonomy to the Jewish nationality in Palestine, freedom of immigration for Jews, and the establishment of a Jewish National Colonizing Corporation for the re-establishment and economic development of the country.
>
> The conditions and forms of the internal autonomy and a Charter for the Jewish National Colonizing Corporation should, in the view of His Majesty's Government, be elaborated in detail and determined with the representatives of the Zionist Organization. [2]

Three months of discussion followed, with the British government trying to reconcile Zionist views with those of British assimilationist Jews, who—like anti-Zionists elsewhere—opposed the Zionist movement on principle. Finally, on November 2, 1917, the British government issued its famous Balfour Declaration, destined to become the foundation stone of Great Power support for Jewish settlement in Palestine.

> His Majesty's Government view with favor the establishment in Palestine of a National Home for the Jewish people, and will use their best endeavors to facilitate the achievement of this object, it being clearly

---

[2] Weizmann, *op. cit.,* p. 203.

understood that nothing shall be done which may prejudice the civil and religious rights of the existing non-Jewish communities in Palestine or the rights and political status enjoyed by Jews in any other country.

This final phrase, "the rights and political status enjoyed by Jews in any other country," was designed to protect assimilationists. The clause just preceding, concerning the "civil and religious rights of the existing non-Jewish communities in Palestine," referred to the indigenous Arabs of the country.

Other British Commitments

Meanwhile, Britain had made two other commitments during the war. One was the secret Sykes-Picot Agreement of 1916, under which France and Britain agreed to parcel out the postwar Middle East. France was to exercise authority in Syria and Lebanon, while Britain was to control Palestine and Iraq. The second commitment was a promise of independence to the Arabs, in return for which Arab leaders would launch a revolt against the Turks. Fruition of this was the Arab Revolt of 1916, conceived and guided by British Arabists in Cairo, attached to the High Commission for Egypt and the Sudan, and led in the field by T. E. Lawrence and other British officers.

These conflicting engagements had been made under the duress of war, when Britain by no means was certain of victory. Postwar analysis showed the three agreements to be incompatible, at least where Palestine was concerned. To be sure Sir Henry McMahon, British High Commissioner in Egypt and chief negotiator with the Arabs, specifically had exempted from the Arab independent state "the districts of Mersin and Alexandretta, and portions of Syria lying to the west of the districts of Damascus, Homs, Hama, and Aleppo." [3] But these exemptions never were agreed to explicitly by Sherif Hussein of Mecca and his sons, Feisal and Abdullah.

The war over, Britain took its three commitments to the peace conference at Paris, bolstered by President Wilson's support in substance of the Balfour Declaration. The new Bolshevik government in Russia, meanwhile, unilaterally had exposed the secret Sykes-Picot agreement between France and Britain. Sherif Hussein, hearing of this treaty for the first time, demanded an explanation from the British. London's reply, dated February 18, 1918, implied that the agreement in no way would interfere with the British promise of an independent state to the Arabs.

At this point President Wilson sent an exploratory commission to the Middle East, composed of Dr. Henry C. King, president of Oberlin College, and Charles Crane, an American industrialist. The report of the King-Crane Commission opposed the creation of a Jewish state in Palestine and recommended instead a unified Syria, embracing Syria, Lebanon, and Palestine. The Arabs themselves, the commissioners reported, favored overwhelmingly an American mandate over the area. A British mandate was second preference, but in no case did the Arabs want French suzerainty. The King-Crane report, bitterly opposed by the Zionists, came to nothing, partly because its issuance coincided with President Wilson's fatal illness.

---

[3] George Antonius, *The Arab Awakening* (Philadelphia: J. B. Lippincott Co., 1939), p. 170.

In Paris, meanwhile, the nub of disagreement centered on Palestine. Both Arabs and Jews believed firmly that the country had been promised to them by the British. The Zionists had the Balfour Declaration to sustain them. The Arabs pointed to the long correspondence between Sherif Hussein and Sir Henry McMahon, which—as the Arabs saw it—clearly had included Palestine within the future Arab kingdom.

In April 1920, mandates were assigned by the Allied Peace Conference, meeting at San Remo. France received a mandate over Syria and Lebanon, as the Sykes-Picot Agreement had foreseen, and Britain acquired control of Palestine and Iraq. The Palestine mandate required the British government to honor its Balfour Declaration, calling for a national homeland for the Jews. Excluded from this requirement was that part of Palestine lying east of the Jordan River, which later became the Amirate of Jordan.

In October 1918 Prince Feisal, third son of Sherif Hussein and commander of Arab armies in the Middle East, had entered Damascus at full gallop at the head of 1,200 tribesmen and had proclaimed an end to Turkish rule. Eighteen months later, on March 8, 1920, a Syrian National Congress meeting in Damascus—convinced by the Paris proceedings that the Arabs had been betrayed—declared the independence of Syria and hailed Feisal as its king. This kingdom was to include Syria and Lebanon, the areas mandated to France.

The French countermanded the Damascus action, deposed Feisal on August 7, 1920, and forced him to flee to the British for protection. The latter installed Feisal as King of Iraq, newly mandated to Britain. Amir Abdullah, Feisal's older brother, threatened to lead his Bedouin troops on Damascus in an effort to restore his brother's throne. As a sop to Abdullah and to prevent trouble with the French, the British carved a new country—Transjordan—out of their mandated territories and gave it to Abdullah to rule. The surrounding Arab lands now had been divided according to Great Power desires. It remained for Britain to reconcile Arabs and Jews within Palestine itself.

Arab Response to Zionism

As early as 1918 the first of a series of meetings had taken place between Prince Feisal and Chaim Weizmann, the two dominant men on the Arab and Jewish sides. At Feisal's war camp east of the Jordan River, Weizmann, traveling under British protection, had tried to convince the Arab leader that Zionist settlement of Palestine would benefit both Semitic peoples, Arabs and Jews. Weizmann returned to England, convinced that Feisal "was in earnest when he said that he was eager to see the Jews and Arabs working in harmony during the Peace Conference which was to come, and that in his view the destiny of the two peoples was linked with the Middle East and must depend on the good will of the Great Powers." [4] T. E. Lawrence, one of Feisal's closest British advisers, confirmed the Amir's sincerity in a letter to Weizmann.

In 1919, during the Paris peace conference, Feisal wrote a letter to Felix Frankfurter, a member of the American Zionist delegation and later an associate justice of the United States Supreme Court.

---

[4] Weizmann, *op. cit.*, p. 235.

We feel that the Arabs and Jews are cousins in race, suffering similar oppressions at the hands of powers stronger than themselves. . . . We Arabs, especially the educated among us, look with the deepest sympathy upon the Zionist movement. Our deputation here in Paris is fully acquainted with the proposals submitted by the Zionist Organization to the Peace Conference, and we regard them as moderate and proper. We will do our best, in so far as we are concerned, to help them through; we will wish the Jews a most hearty welcome home.

With the chiefs of your movement, especially with Dr. Weizmann, we have had, and continue to have, the closest relations. He has been a great helper of our cause, and I hope the Arabs may soon be in a position to make the Jews some return for their kindness. We are working together for a reformed and revived Near East, and our two movements complete one another . . . there is room in Syria for us both. Indeed, I think that neither can be a real success without the other. [5]

This apparent identity of views was climaxed by an accord signed by Feisal and Weizmann on January 3, 1919, of which the key paragraphs read as follows:

In the establishment of the Constitution and Administration of Palestine, all such measures shall be adopted as will afford the fullest guarantees for carrying into effect the British Government's Declaration of November 2nd, 1917 (the Balfour Declaration).

All necessary measures shall be taken to encourage and stimulate immigration of Jews into Palestine on a large scale, and as quickly as possible to settle Jewish immigrants upon the land through closer settlement and intensive cultivation of the soil. In taking such measures the Arab peasant and tenant farmers shall be protected in their rights, and shall be assisted in forwarding their economic development. [6]

Given this promising beginning, what went wrong that has produced an Arab-Jewish confrontation, ever more dangerous to world peace, and to which no end is in sight? Clearly Weizmann and Feisal were talking about different things. The Zionists had in mind the creation of a Jewish political state in Palestine, within which the rights of Arab citizens would be protected. Feisal and the Arabs foresaw Jewish immigration within the framework of Arab political control. Palestine, in the Arab view, was to form part of Feisal's greater Arab kingdom—the independent state promised by the British. Indeed, Feisal stipulated that his accord with Weizmann would be null and void if the British reneged on granting Arab independence.

This basic misunderstanding, coupled with the ouster of Feisal from Damascus by the French, virtually guaranteed strife in the Holy Land, during the period of Britain's mandate. There is little need here to catalogue the successive acts of terrorism by which Arabs and Jews violated each other's communities during these troubled years, except to say that bitterness had reached the explosion point by the time Britain ended its mandate in May 1948.

Successively the British reinterpreted their mandate, in the hope of bringing peace to Palestine. A White Paper of 1922 assured the Arabs that the purpose of Jewish settlement was not to make Palestine "as Jewish as England is English," but to create a Jewish community, based on religion and race, toward which Jews

[5] *Ibid.*, pp. 245-46.
[6] *Ibid.*, p. 247.

throughout the world could look with pride. Immigration, the White Paper stressed, would be limited to the absorptive capacity of the country.

The British sought in vain to draw Arabs and Jews into the government of Palestine. A plan for a Legislative Council, in which Arab and Jewish members would assist the High Commissioner, collapsed when the Arabs refused to take part. Major riots in 1929, triggered by a dispute over holy places centering on the Wailing Wall in Jerusalem, caused the British to issue a new White Paper the following year.

This document declared that the economic situation in Palestine required Jewish immigration to be suspended and the purchase of land by Jews to be restricted. Protests by Zionists throughout the world caused the British government to reverse itself. Prime Minister Ramsay MacDonald, in a letter to Chaim Weizmann dated February 13, 1931, pledged that establishment of a Jewish national home in Palestine remained a positive task of His Majesty's government.

The years that followed saw a rising flow of Jewish immigrants to Palestine, until, by the end of 1936, nearly 30 percent of the country's population was Jewish. This compared to 13 percent at the time of the 1922 census. Yearly figures of immigration were as follows:

1930	4,944
1931	4,075
1932	9,553
1933	30,327
1934	42,359
1935	61,864
1936	29,727
Total for 7-year period:	182,849[7]

Jewish Agency in Palestine

Article 4 of the mandate provided for a Jewish Agency, designed to cooperate with British officials in implementing the Jewish national homeland in Palestine. The President of the Jewish Agency, which became the official spokesman of world Jewry concerning immigration to the Holy Land, was president of the World Zionist Organization. Except for the years 1931-35, these twin posts were held by Dr. Weizmann. The Jewish Agency examined candidates for immigration and granted them certificates of eligibility, with which would-be immigrants applied to British consulates for visas. Within Palestine, a standing executive committee of the Jewish Agency was headed by David Ben-Gurion, later the first prime minister of Israel. The foreign department of the executive committee was directed by Moshe Shertok (Sharett), who became Ben-Gurion's foreign minister.[8]

Apart from the Jewish Agency, the Jewish community in Palestine had its own internal organization, with limited rights of self-government. There was an elected Assembly, made up of representatives of a number of Jewish political parties,

---

[7] *The Political History of Palestine Under British Administration, op. cit.,* p. 15.
[8] See George Lenczowski, *The Middle East in World Affairs* (Ithaca, New York: Cornell University Press, Second Edition, 1956), pp. 317-18.

foreshadowing the political alignment which would emerge with statehood. Also part of the Jewish community organization was a General Council (Vaad Leumi), standing in the same relationship to the Assembly as a cabinet to parliament.

Economic activities of the community were administered by the Histadruth, or Jewish Federation of Labor, divided politically along the same lines as the Jewish community as a whole. More than a collection of trade unions, Histadruth controlled a host of industrial enterprises, organized the marketing activities of kibbutzim, and ran schools and hospitals. Jewish education flourished and in 1925 the Hebrew University was opened in Jerusalem under the leadership of Dr. Judah L. Magnes.

Arab Community of Palestine

The tightly-organized Jewish community, in other words, possessed a shadow government, administering the political, economic, social, and education needs of the Yishuv, or Jewish community in Palestine. The Arabs of Palestine were poorly equipped to compete with this Jewish organizational effort. The Jewish community had a democratic structure. The Arab community was split along traditional lines, with an oligarchy of wealthy landowners and aristrocratic Arab families standing apart from the mass of Arab peasantry.

It was this oligarchy, conceiving of Palestine's future in its own terms—i.e., a semifeudal society—which refused to cooperate with the mandatory power and with the Jews in governing the country. Arab leadership rejected a British offer to create an Arab Agency, analogous to the Jewish Agency, even though this proposed agency would have had a voice in controlling Jewish immigration.

Dominating the Arab community in Palestine was Haj Amin el-Husseini, Grand Mufti of Jerusalem and the leader of Arab traditionalists who opposed both the British and the Jews. A rival Arab political group headed by Raghib Bey Nashashibi wanted to broaden Arab education, introduce social reforms, and cooperate to some extent with the British. Within the Arab Executive, however, elected by the Palestine Arab Congress, Haj Amin's conservatives submerged Arab liberals. This remained true after 1936, when the Arab Executive gave way to the Arab Higher Committee, formed by the merger of five out of six Arab political parties.

The structural difference between the two communities, Arab and Jewish, cannot be overstressed. Had ordinary Arabs been able to participate directly in their political affairs, as did their Jewish counterparts, the history of Palestine might have turned out differently. But a major aim of Palestine's Arab leadership was to prevent the Zionists, or the British, from upsetting the long-established semifeudalism of Arab society.

Wealthy Arab landowners, not peasants or tenant farmers, sold the land of Palestine to Jews. Powerful groups of Jewish settlers, backed by the financial resources of the Jewish National Fund, offered high prices for land. There are Arabs of standing in Lebanon today, whose fortunes were based on land sales to Zionists. Often these were not prime fields, as Arabs later were to charge, but marshy malarial tracts, which Jewish settlers had to clear at their peril, before kibbutzim could be founded. Even those British officials in Palestine who sympathized

23

with the Arabs, and there were many, conceded that by no means were Zionists buying up the best land in the country.

Arab Rebellion

Repeatedly, in the mid-1930s Arab political leaders demanded a halt to Jewish immigration and an end to land sales to Jews. In 1935 the mandate government offered a new Legislative Council for Palestine, weighted in favor of the Arabs. The British government in London ruled that the proposal was inconsistent with Britain's mandate responsibilities toward the Jews and the plan was dropped.

By now Arab anger was expressing itself in mounting violence, characterized by labor strikes, the killing of Jews and destruction of their property, and the hurling of bombs in towns. The period from 1936 to 1939 became known as the Arab Rebellion. More than 3,000 persons were killed during the rebellion, many of them Arab guerrillas shot by British troops. Power within the mandate government shifted progressively from civil to military hands. The Arab Higher Committee was declared illegal and its leaders deported to the Seychelles. Haj Amin el-Husseini escaped to Lebanon, where he continued to direct the rebellion.

A feature of this period was the assignment of Orde Wingate, a young pro-Zionist British officer, to train Jewish guerrilla forces, or Special Night Squads, to combat Arab resistance fighters. Wingate's men became the shock troops of the Jewish Haganah, a self-defense organization established to protect the kibbutzim.

The fury of the rebellion brought forth the first of many partition schemes, destined to dot Palestine's diplomatic history. In 1937 the British proposed dividing the country into a Jewish state, an Arab state, and a neutral enclave around Jerusalem and Bethlehem, to remain under British jurisdiction. The Arabs rejected the scheme, while the Twentieth Zionist Congress agreed to negotiate with the British on the terms of partition. Ultimately the plan was condemned as unworkable, by a partition commission headed by Sir John Woodhead.

A revised partition scheme advanced by Woodhead was turned down by the British government. In 1939, searching for a compromise solution, the British government convened an Arab-Jewish conference in London. Arab delegates, representing Palestine, Transjordan, Iraq, Egypt, Saudi Arabia, and Yemen, refused to sit at the same table with Zionists. British officials were forced to talk separately with each side.

The conference, which lasted from February 7 to March 15, 1939, ended in failure. The Arabs insisted on an independent Arab Palestine and an end to Jewish immigration. The Zionists wanted unlimited immigration and their own Jewish state. On May 17 of that year the British produced another White Paper, calling for an independent Palestinian state to be created in ten years, linked by special treaty with Britain. The country was divided into three zones, in one of which land transfers from Arabs to Jews were to be allowed. In a second zone land transfers would be restricted and in the third area they would be forbidden. Jewish immigration was to be limited to a total of 75,000 over the next five years.

The Arabs rejected this proposal as not going far enough. But more meaningful opposition came from the Zionists, who charged the British with reversing the

24

policy of the mandate. The Permanent Mandates Commission of the League of Nations supported the Zionist view.

The outbreak of World War II and Nazi persecution of the Jews changed the context of the Palestine conflict. Though angered by the White Paper of 1939, Zionist leaders saw clearly that the salvation of the Jewish people depended on Allied victory over the Axis powers. The Jewish Agency called on all Jews to cooperate with Britain in the prosecution of the war and 27,000 Jews volunteered for service with British auxiliary forces in Palestine. (Twelve thousand Palestine Arabs also volunteered for British service.) In 1944 a Jewish Brigade Group was formed, which participated in the last stages of the Allied campaign in Italy.

Nonetheless, British mandate authorities implemented the 1939 White Paper, by dividing Palestine into three land transfer zones. Thousands of Jews fleeing Hitler's Third Reich were refused entry to Palestine, on the grounds that Axis agents might be among them and that the refugees had not gone through the established screening process. "Illegal" immigrants were interned on Cyprus or Mauritius, or were forced to wander the Mediterranean Sea in inadequate ships. World attention was drawn to their plight, when the immigrant ship *Struma* sank off the Turkish coast, after being refused permission to dock in Palestine.

American Zionist Activity

On May 11, 1942, the American Zionist Organization—convinced that the British would adopt the 1939 White Paper as policy after the war—accepted the so-called Biltmore Program, drafted by David Ben-Gurion in Palestine. This called for establishment of a Jewish state including all of Palestine, creation of a Jewish Army, scrapping of the White Paper, and unlimited Jewish immigration. This program became official policy of the World Zionist Organization.

In Palestine itself, meanwhile, wartime cooperation between the Jews and the British began to falter. Two Jewish extremist groups, the Stern Gang—founded by a Polish Jew named Abraham Stern—and the Irgun Zvai Leumi, launched terrorist attacks on British installations. In November 1944 two members of the Stern Gang assassinated Lord Moyne, British Minister of State in the Middle East, in Cairo. These acts of terrorism were denounced by Zionist officials, in and out of Palestine.

American Zionists during the war had sought to lay the political groundwork for United States support of the Zionist cause. A number of state legislatures passed pro-Zionist resolutions and President Roosevelt issued a statement favoring Zionist aspirations.

On August 31, 1945, President Truman urged British Prime Minister Clement R. Attlee to admit immediately 100,000 Jewish refugees to Palestine. This appeal, both humanitarian and political in inspiration, offered the British no help in getting the Arabs of Palestine to agree. In reply, London proposed formation of an Anglo-American Committee of Inquiry to study the problem. The upshot was a unanimous report, dated April 20, 1946, containing three major recommendations. The British mandate should be continued, until a new trusteeship arrangement could be worked out by the United Nations. One hundred thousand Jewish victims of "Nazi and Fascist persecution" should be allowed to enter Palestine. The land transfer regulations should be rescinded.

Rather than accept or reject this report, the British and American governments appointed higher officials to a new study commission. This higher body revived the old British proposal for a partitioned Palestine, with future Jewish immigration to be made dependent on Arab-Jewish agreement. President Truman's response was to urge again that 100,000 Jewish refugees be allowed to enter Palestine.

This second appeal, dated October 4, 1946, reflected the degree to which Zionism had infiltrated internal American politics. An election campaign was underway in New York, with two Democrats—James M. Mead and Herbert Lehman—facing an uphill battle for election as governor and senator of the state. Both men called on the White House for a pro-Zionist statement, on the grounds that Thomas Dewey, the Republican candidate for governor, was about to make one. Both political parties evidently assumed that New York Jews would vote in a bloc for whichever candidate appeared to support Zionist aims. Following President Truman's second appeal to Mr. Attlee, Mr. Dewey issued a statement, declaring that "not 100,000 but several hundreds of thousands" of Jews should be admitted to Palestine.[9]

Britain by now was making a final effort to bring Arabs and Jews together in a conference. Convened in London on September 9, 1946, the meeting was to consider the practical consequences of partitioning Palestine. The Zionists refused to attend, as did leaders of the Arab Palestine community. Only delegates of the newly-formed Arab League took part and they repeated the Arab refusal to accept any partition of the Holy Land.

United Nations Enters the Scene

No longer could Britain hope to hammer out a Palestine solution acceptable to the two peoples, Arabs and Jews, who had to live there when the mandate power had departed. British officials also felt themselves besieged by gratuitous—and oft times politically motivated—advice as to what course the mandate power should pursue. This coincided with a progressive rundown of British responsibilities generally in the Mediterranean area, stemming from Britain's wartime exhaustion. Finally the British government felt impelled to broaden responsibility for the tangled Palestine question by calling in the United Nations.

Thus began the United Nations' long, dramatic, and traumatic confrontation with the Arab-Jewish conflict. A special session of the General Assembly, called for by Britain, established in May 1947 an 11-nation United Nations Special Committee on Palestine (UNSCOP). The report of this body, following a visit to Palestine, proposed the creation of an independent and economically unified Palestine as soon as possible, with the United Nations to assume a supervisory role in the interim.

The UNSCOP report then divided into majority and minority recommendations. The majority plan (Canada, Czechoslovakia, Guatemala, The Netherlands, Peru, Sweden, and Uruguay) recommended the division of Palestine into a Jewish state,

---

[9] *New York Times,* October 7, 1946.

an Arab state, and an internationalized Jerusalem. The minority report (India, Iran, and Yugoslavia) suggested a federated Palestine, with Arab and Jewish communities exercising local autonomy. Jewish immigration should be allowed for three years, up to the absorptive capacity of the Jewish canton. (The eleventh member of UNSCOP was Australia.)

The Zionists, though not enthusiastic, endorsed the majority report. The Arabs opted for the minority plan, since it provided for a single Palestinian state, dominated by Arabs and with a termination to Jewish immigration. A straw vote, taken during the debate which followed, indicated that the necessary two-thirds majority for partition could not be mustered. American Zionists swung into action, focusing on six nations which had opposed partition. These were Haiti, Liberia, Greece, Ethiopia, Nationalist China, and the Philippines. Telegrams and telephone calls from well-known Americans urged the governments of these six nations to reverse their votes.

"An ex-Governor," wrote Kermit Roosevelt, "a prominent Democrat with White House and other connections, personally telephoned Haiti urging that its delegation be instructed to change its vote. . . . A well-known economist also close to the White House, and acting in a liaison capacity for the Zionist organization, exerted his powers of persuasion upon the Liberian delegate." [10]

Four of the target states—Haiti, Liberia, Ethiopia, and the Philippines—reversed their votes. China abstained, while Greece stuck to its convictions. On November 29, 1947, the United Nations voted that Palestine should be partitioned. Thirty-three nations voted for, 13 against, and ten abstained. Britain, as the mandatory power, abstained. The United States, the Soviet Union, and France approved partition.

Bands of armed Arabs, mainly from inside the Holy Land but also from surrounding areas, began to attack Jewish settlements. Jewish activists replied with violence against the Arabs. Casualties mounted and Britain, foreseeing no solution to the impasse, ended its mandate over Palestine on May 14, 1948.

The same day the Zionists proclaimed the establishment of the state of Israel. The first government to recognize Israel was the United States, followed closely by the Soviet Union and by the United Nations itself. One day later, the armies of five Arab nations—Egypt, Transjordan, Iraq, Syria, and Lebanon—invaded Palestine to prevent the establishment of a Jewish state.

---

[10] *Kermit Roosevelt,* "The Partition of Palestine: A Lesson in Pressure Politics," *The Middle East Journal,* January 1948, p. 15.

IV. ISRAEL AND THE ARABS

E ver since May 15, 1948, Israel and the Arabs have been technically at war. Seen from the perspective of the past 22 years, this state of affairs has been marked by three major clashes and innumerable smaller battles, centered on the Jordanian and Egyptian fronts. At this writing scarcely a day passes without fighting of some kind across the Suez Canal or the Jordan River or the western slopes of Mount Herman in Lebanese territory.

War Number One: 1948

The first Arab-Israeli war produced a shock from which the Arabs never truly have recovered—their defeat at the hands of the numerically inferior Jews. The David and Goliath simile, often used to describe the Semitic confrontation, is correct from the standpoint of numbers. The Arab states involved, with about 40 million citizens, possessed regular armies totaling approximately 170,000 men. Against this the infant Israeli state, with fewer than one million Jews, had the self-defense organization Haganah. The two extremist groups, the Sern Gang and Irgun Zvai Leumi, at first were a problem, rather than a help. They refused to serve under Haganah's command and at times had to be subdued by force by Haganah troops.

But Arab numerical superiority, plus fidelity to Islam and common use of the Arabic language, did not help the Arabs to wage war. Torn by dynastic rivalries, the Arabs never placed their armies under effective joint command. Often Arab units in the line were given faulty equipment and had no sense of unified support from their governments at home. Most Arab soldiers involved never had seen Palestine and were far more concerned with scrabbling out a hard living at home than with the plight of Arabs in the Holy Land.

Jewish soldiers, by contrast, had their backs to the sea, with fresh memories of the Nazi terror in Europe. Furthermore, they had a military tradition dating back to 1920, when Haganah ("defense") was founded. Under the impulse of Arab guerrilla attacks on Jewish communities, like those in 1929 on the Jewish parts of Jerusalem, Hebron, and Safad, Haganah came to embrace the entire Yishuv, with

29

almost every Jewish man belonging to it. Though technically illegal during the mandate, Haganah in fact became a tightly-disciplined fighting force, with a central authority to direct training and to purchase arms.

This was capped by British training during World War II, when Haganah decided which Jews would volunteer for service with British forces and which would remain at home. Orde Wingate's training of Jewish night-fighting units has been mentioned. Finally, when Rommel's forces were advancing across North Africa, the British trained Jewish shock troops, called Palmach, to act as guerrillas, should the Germans invade Palestine.

The war began on May 15, 1948, in an atmosphere of bitterness and terror, caused in part by the cold-blooded massacre of innocent Arab men, women, and children of the village of Deir Yasin by the Irgun Zvai Leumi on April 9. During the fighting nearly one million Palestine Arabs—the exact number is in dispute— fled or were driven from their homes into surrounding Arab lands. Some fled at the urging of Arab leaders, who, confident of ultimate victory, wanted to clear the fighting zones of civilians. Other Arabs panicked, afraid of Jewish reprisals. Some Israeli units drove Arabs from their homes and then razed their villages.

The Lebanese and Syrian armies attacked from the north and northeast, aided by a volunteer force called the Arab Liberation Army, commanded by Fawzi al-Kawukji. Transjordan's British-trained Arab Legion attacked from the east, as did the army of Iraq, which traveled overland across hundreds of miles of desert to reach the fighting front. Egypt commanded the southern Arab front and Saudi Arabia sent a token force.

In the initial stages of fighting the Jews seized Haifa and Jaffa on the Mediterranean coast and Tiberias and Safad in Galilee. Arab attacks generally ground to a halt. But the Arab Legion, commanded by the British Glubb Pasha, clung stubbornly to Old Jerusalem, while the Israelis won the western part of the city, or New Jerusalem.

On May 20, meanwhile, the U.N. Security Council appointed Swedish Count Folke Bernadotte to be United Nations Mediator for Palestine. On June 11 Bernadotte secured a truce and the fighting stopped for four weeks. During this period the mediator proposed a federation of Palestine and Jordan, to include an Arab and a Jewish state. Both sides rejected the plan and fighting broke out again July 9, with Israeli forces regrouped and freshly equipped with weapons bought in Czechoslovakia, France, and elsewhere.

In the next ten days the Israelis forced Arab armies to retreat, except for the Arab Legion, which still held Old Jerusalem and the town of Latrun. A second truce, which began on July 18, was used by Bernadotte to recommend a revised partition plan to the U.N. General Assembly. Under this plan the Arabs would have received the Negev Desert, thus affording Egypt a land link to Jordan. On September 17, 1948, Count Bernadotte was assassinated by Jewish terrorists in Jerusalem. This act, though repudiated by responsible Israeli leaders, signaled Jewish determination to hold the Negev for future settlement.

Fighting began again on October 14 and the Israeli army cleared Galilee of Arab troops, drove briefly into Lebanon, and in the south captured El Auja on the Palestine-Egyptian frontier. Israel then emptied the Negev of Egyptian troops and advanced to Eilat on the Gulf of Aqaba. The shooting war stopped on January 7, 1949, with Israel, as we have seen, holding over 30 percent more territory than had been assigned to the Jewish state by the U.N. partition plan.[1]

From January to July 1949, Dr. Ralph Bunche, successor to Count Bernadotte, negotiated armistice agreements on the island of Rhodes between Israel and four Arab states—Egypt, Lebanon, Jordan, and Syria. Iraq, having no contiguous borders with Palestine, refused to sign an armistice and still has not done so. Egypt held the Gaza Strip, King Abdullah had annexed the West Bank, and the armistice lines of 1949 took on the appearance of permanent frontiers. U.N. Mixed Armistice Commissions, each comprising Arab and Israeli officers and a neutral chairman, were created to police the uneasy borders. The United Nations Relief and Works Agency for Palestine Refugees in the Near East (UNRWA) came into being to minster to Arabs who had lost their homes.

Between the Wars

Frontier inequities were inevitable, since the borders had been drawn—not according to economic sense—but where the armies stood. In some cases the houses of Arab villagers remained in Jordan, while their farmlands fell to Israel. One such town was Qalqilya, backed up against the Samarian hills. Overnight the people of Qalqilya lost their livelihood, because their flourishing orange groves, stretching across the coastal plain toward the Mediterranean Sea, were awarded to Israel. Not surprisingly, the men of Qalqilya took to infiltrating across the armistice line to steal fruit—or, from their point of view, to take what rightfully belonged to them. Pilferage grew into sabotage and, finally, to the killing of Jews.

The Israeli army in turn mounted reprisal raids across the border, which the Jordanian government was powerless to prevent. Seeking to halt these reprisals, Jordan clamped down hard on infiltrators, arresting dozens of Qalqilyans. Yet, so pervasive was the Arab refusal to negotiate with the Jews, that Jordan in 1952 turned down an Israeli offer to give back Qalqilya's lands, in return for Jordanian territory around the Dead Sea.[2]

In another border village I saw Arab children on the Israeli side, watching Arab children playing marbles on the Jordanian side. Occasionally a marble rolled under the barbed wire frontier and was tossed back by a child, while Jewish and Arab police patrolled impassively up and down.

On the night of October 14, 1953, a battalion of the Israeli army swept across the frontier and killed more than 50 Arab men, women, and children in the Jordanian village of Qibya. For this raid Israel was condemned by the U.N. Security Council. Israeli officials claimed in defense that the number of Arabs killed in the raid had been fewer than the number of Jews killed in recent months by infiltrators from Jordan. A second major Israeli raid, to avenge an Arab attack on an Israeli bus at Scorpion Pass, took place against Nahhalin in March 1954. On the

---

[1] A detailed account of the 1948 war, from the Jordanian point of view, is given by Sir John Bagot Glubb, *A Soldier with the Arabs* (New York: Harper & Brothers Publishers, 1957).

[2] For a study of Qalqilya's plight, and that of the Israeli kibbutz farming Qalqilya's lands, see Harry B. Ellis, *Israel and the Middle East* (New York: The Ronald Press Company, 1957), chapters 1, 7, and 8.

night of October 11, 1956, Israeli troops killed approximately 25 citizens of Qal-qilya, which the Israelis claimed had become a center of organized infiltration.

To the north, meanwhile, Syrian artillery on the Golan Heights had been sniping persistently at Israeli fishing boats on the Sea of Galilee. In reprisal, Israeli units stormed the Heights on December 11, 1955, and killed 49 Syrians. Stung by a Security Council condemnation of this raid, Israelis retorted that 25 times, at least, Syrian guns had fired on Israeli boats during the preceding year.

Syria did not deny the charge but claimed that Israeli boats had been operating illegally on water that was no-man's-land. The firing, from the Syrian point of view, had been provoked by this incursion. Israel insisted its fishermen stayed on the Israeli side of the Galilean Sea.

The frontier with Egypt also was unquiet. Arab infiltrators from Gaza had begun to mine Israeli roads and blow up water pipelines and bridges. This campaign was military in nature, as opposed to the sabotage, pilferage, and acts of murder committed by individual marauders from Jordan. In February 1955 Israel struck back at the Egyptian army in Gaza, killing 38 Egyptian soldiers. President Nasser later claimed it was this raid which persuaded him finally of Israel's aggressive intentions and propelled his search for foreign arms. A second Israeli attack drove Egyptian troops from occupation of the El Auja demilitarized zone.

Egypt's response was to organize selected fedayeen, or commandos, and send them into Israel to commit sabotage and to kill. These raiders, under the overall command of Col. Mustapha Hafiz of the Egyptian army, operated first from Gaza and Sinai and later from bases in Syria and Jordan.

War Number Two: 1956

The accumulated tensions and bitterness of eight years of punctuated armistice now exploded into fresh warfare. On October 29, 1956, 32,000 soldiers of the Israeli army invaded the Sinai Peninsula and in seven days had reached the Suez Canal. The Gaza Strip and Sinai itself were emptied of Egyptian troops and of fedayeen bases. Israeli soldiers looked out from sand dunes on the East Bank onto the historic canal, which had been denied to Israeli flag ships since the creaton of the Jewish state.

Israel's action was taken in secret concert with the governments of France and Britain, whose object was to recapture the Suez Canal, nationalized by President Nasser on July 26, 1956. On October 31, while Israeli and Egyptian tanks battled in Sinai, French and British aircraft based on Cyprus began to bomb Egypt, in prelude to invasion. Swiftly the United Nations achieved a cease-fire and demanded the evacuation of invading troops. In December 1956 France and Britain, under intense pressure from the United States, the Soviet Union, and the United Nations, withdrew their last forces from Egypt.

Israel proved more stubborn. Conquest of Sinai, to Israelis, had meant pacification of the southern frontier, peace for kibbutzim near Gaza, and free passage through the Gulf of Aqaba to and from the port of Eilat. But Israel could not hold out against the threat of economic sanctions from Washington. Under the Trading with the Enemy Act of 1941 and the Export Control Act of 1949, President Eisenhower had authority to halt, not only official American aid to Israel, but private donations by American Jews. In March 1957 the last Israeli units filed out of Sinai. Economic sanctions, Prime Minister Ben-Gurion told his people, would render impossible Israel's continuing mission to gather in the exiles.

Meanwhile, a United Nations Emergency Force (UNEF), made up of troops from neutral nations, took up positions at the southern tip of the Sinai Peninsula and along the Gaza frontier. The troops were positioned on the Egyptian sides of the lines after Israel refused to allow UNEF forces on territory it held. No longer would Egyptian guns planted at Sharm al-Sheik and on the tiny islands of Tiran and Sanafir threaten Israeli shipping in the Strait of Tiran. Eilat began to boom, as an outlet for Israeli exports to East Africa and Asia and as a port of entry for oil from Iran. The Israeli government warned that removal of UNEF from Sharm al-Sheik would constitute an act of war.

The Suez Canal issue was more complicated. Long months of labor and millions of dollars were spent to clear the waterway of sunken ships, scuttled by Egypt during the Suez war. Then, without fanfare, Egypt began to allow Israeli cargoes on non-Israeli flag ships to transit the canal. More than 40 such cargoes passed safely through, by Israeli count.

In March 1959 the Egyptian government halted even this "invisible" kind of passage. Cairo's action appeared to flout three legal documents—the Constantinople Convention of 1888; a Security Council resolution dated September 1, 1951, urging Egypt to open the canal to all shipping; and Cairo's own declaration of April 24, 1957, promising to respect the Constantinople Convention.

The latter document was open to contradictory interpretation. Egypt cited Article 10 of the Constantinople Convention, which provides that freedom of passage "shall not interfere with measures Egypt might find necessary to take to secure the defense of Egypt." By Cairo's lights, therefore, Egypt was not reversing its declared willingness to abide by the convention.

U.N. Secretary General Dag Hammarskjold, in separate talks with each side, finally worked out the following compromise:

1. Israeli cargoes could pass through the Suez canal if:
   a. There was no publication by Israel of their movement.
   b. They were carried in non-Israeli flag ships, though the vessels might be chartered by Israel.
2. It was also stipulated that cargoes leaving Israel must be F.O.B. (free on board), meaning that ownership had passed to the purchaser by the time the cargoes went through the canal.
3. Cargoes inbound for Israel must be carried C.I.F. (cost, freight, insurance), meaning the cargo still was owned by the nation exporting it to Israel. [3]

This formula, too, was voided by President Nasser. In December 1959 Egypt halted the Greek ship *Astypalea,* bound for Djibouti with a cargo of Israeli cement. This seizure followed the earlier detention at Port Said of the Danish freighter *Inge Toft,* headed for the Far East with Israeli freight. Hammarskjold's efforts to revive the formula proved futile. Eventually both ships unloaded their freight at Port Said and sailed away. Since then no Israeli cargoes are known to have moved through the Suez Canal.

---

[3] Harry B. Ellis, *Challenge in the Middle East* (New York: The Ronald Press Company, 1960) p. 101.

War Number Three: 1967

The decade following the Suez war of 1956 witnessed a mushrooming growth of Soviet influence in the Middle East. Moscow sold hundreds of millions of dollars worth of jet aircraft, tanks, rockets, and other weapons to the United Arab Republic, Syria, and—after the 1958 revolution in Baghdad—to Iraq. Modernization of their armies increased Arab willingness to challenge Israel and Arab confidence that the defeats suffered in the first two rounds of fighting could be reversed.

Primary threat to Israel came from the build-up of Egyptian land and air forces in Sinai. By the spring of 1967 most of the Egyptian army was stationed in Sinai and bases of the Egyptian air force ringed Cairo and the Suez Canal. Other UAR aircraft, plus Soviet SAM-2 (surface-to-air) missiles, were in Sinai itself.

President Nasser has since denied that he had plans to attack Israel. "In fact," declared Nasser, "three of our best divisions were in Yemen at the time, and if we had been preparing for an attack, it would have been logical to bring them home first." [4] But the Egyptian leader apparently did foresee the danger of war in the growing confrontation between Israel and Syria. Warlike noises in Damascus and repeated shelling of Israeli settlements from the Golan Heights had notched tension high on the northern front. "What I did say, however," added Nasser, "was that if they attacked Syria, we would retaliate by attacking them." [5]

At this point Nasser ordered UNEF out of Sharm al-Sheik and Sinai and declared a blockade of the Strait of Tiran to Israeli shipping. This was in May 1967. Israel's problem then was to determine what strategy to pursue, based on the assumption that war was inevitable. Should the Jewish state wage a preventive war or wait for the Arabs to strike first? Just prior to the June war Israel's Air Force was outnumbered 2½-to-1 by planes of the Egyptian air force. [6] Furthermore, Israeli airfields were few and vulnerable to attack. The generals argued that Egypt's air force must be neutralized in a pre-emptive blow, to free Israeli aircraft to cover the advance of ground troops and to prevent bombing and strafing attacks on Israeli bases and towns.

This strategy was adopted. On the morning of June 5 Israeli French-built jets streaked across the Mediterranean and over Sinai at low level and blasted the UAR air force into ruins on the ground. The same day the Israeli army rolled across the frontier into Gaza and into Sinai at El Arish and farther south. Israel now sent a message to King Hussein, through Lt. Gen. Odd Bull, Norwegian commander of U.N. peace-keeping forces in Palestine. Israel, the message stated, did not intend to attack Jordan. The king should stay out of the war.

King Hussein, in what turned out to be the most costly mistake of his career, disregarded Israeli advice and ordered his air force and artillery into action. Hussein may have disbelieved Israeli sincerity. Or, more likely, he was swayed by a telephone message he had received from President Nasser in Cairo. Nasser told the

---

[4] *Newsweek International Edition,* February 10, 1969, p. 26.
[5] *Ibid.,* p. 26.
[6] Geoffrey Kemp, *Arms & Security: The Egypt-Israel Case* (London: The Institute for Strategic Studies, Adelphi Papers, Number Fifty-Two, October 1968), p. 5.

king that, at the very moment their voices were crackling on the wire, UAR planes were in action over Israel. Jordan should join the fight and press on with Egypt to final victory. At the time Nasser spoke, his once-proud Soviet-built air force lay smoking on the desert. No Egyptian planes were over Israel.

Egyptians since have led Jordan to believe that Nasser did not know the extent of the disaster at the time he spoke. This theory was discounted by an elder Jordanian statesman, who had served both King Abdullah and his grandson Hussein. "We received word from Boumedienne," the Jordanian told me, "that Nasser already had reported the Egyptian Air Force was destroyed, before Nasser spoke with Hussein. If Algiers had heard the truth, why not Amman?" (Houari Boumedienne is President of Algeria.)

"Or the king may have reasoned another way," continued the Jordanian. "If he did not go in, he faced possible overthrow or assassination by the Palestinian element of Jordan's population. This would have given Israel an excuse to intervene to restore order. Either way," the elder statesman shrugged, "Hussein would have lost."

Jordan's army was decimated, as was the Jordanian air force. Israeli tank commanders, crawling along the roads in bitterly-contested battles toward Nablus and Jenin, saluted the courage of Jordanian soldiers, many of whom died in their tanks rather than surrender. Lost to Jordan was Old Jerusalem and all the West Bank. Unlike President Nasser, King Hussein has been unable to restore Jordan's fighting forces to their former level of equipment.

On the sixth day of the war, with Israeli troops at the Suez Canal and the Gulf of Suez, and with the West Bank under Jewish control, Israel turned to the Golan Heights and Syria. By nightfall of June 10 the hills had been secured and the six-day blitzkrieg was over.

Post-1967

Three years have passed since the end of the war. Two new problems have evolved in the Arab world. The first is that although, formerly, the Arab nations were concerned with regaining the lost parts of Palestine and restoring the refugees to their homes, they are now equally concerned with getting their *own* lands back. The second concerns the growing influence and power of the different Palestinian commando groups throughout the Arab world. This latter problem, which will be discussed later on in the chapter, has proved to be an enigma not only to Israel but oftentimes to the Arab nations as well.

In order to assist the Arabs in regaining lost territories, the Soviet Union made a calculated decision after the June war to re-equip Egyptian forces. Virtually all major items of equipment, including aircraft, tanks, artillery pieces, and various types of rockets, including SAM-3 missiles, have been supplied. Thousands of Soviet military advisers now are in the United Arab Republic. Whether they are there to discourage the Egyptians from starting a new war, or simply to restrain them until Egyptian troops have mastered their complex equipment, is not clear. Moscow is believed to want no large-scale Arab-Jewish confrontation that might drag in the great powers.

On May Day 1969 President Nasser declared in a speech that the Arabs would accept peace only on the basis of the November 1967 U.N. resolution, calling for Israeli withdrawal from occupied lands. Egypt now considered itself justified, Nasser added, in attacking Israeli civilian targets.[7] Earlier the UAR government verbally had placed the cease-fire line in mid-Sinai, not on the Suez Canal. This meant, from Cairo's point of view, that Egyptian bombardment of Israeli positions on the East Bank did not violate the U.N.-sponsored truce.[8] Still earlier, on April 23, 1969, an Egyptian government spokesman affirmed that, in any case, Egypt regarded the 1967 cease-fire agreement with Israel as null and void, because Israel had not accepted the U.N. resolution of November 1967.[9]

All this strengthens Israeli determination to stay on the Suez Canal, at least until the Arabs agree to negotiate peace directly with the Jews. From the Israeli point of view, to rereat now without the security of a peace agreement, would bring into being the same kind of dangerous situation that had prevailed in May 1967.

General Dayan forecast Israeli offensive action across the cease-fire lines, if the Arabs in general and Egyptians in particular continued their attacks. "The question," declared the Israeli minister of defense, "is not whether we have it in our power to capture additional territory. We can reach Amman and Damascus in one breakthrough. The problem is whether we can continue to hold on to the cease-fire lines in a war of attrition against artillery fire and commando raids, not only for days and weeks, but maybe even for months and years. . . . We must reply with a fighting refusal to any effort to push us off the cease-fire lines, while at the same time pursuing a constructive policy in the occupied areas by the establishment of Jewish settlements." [10]

This description of the establishment of Jewish settlements as a "constructive task," implies that General Dayan opposes Israeli withdrawal from occupied territories. Otherwise, what would happen to the kibbutzim now being built in Syria and Jordan? Israeli spokesmen admit freely to the presence of Jewish settlers on the Golan Heights and the West Bank. But no kibbutzim, an Israeli official told me, have been established in the Sinai Peninsula, nor in Gaza.

Old Arab Demands

Preoccupation with Israel's latest territorial gains does not mean the Arabs have forgotten their old demands, relating directly to Palestine. At the heart of these is insistence that all Arab refugees be given a free choice to return to their Palestine homes or receive compensation for their loss. This demand is rooted in U.N. General Assembly resolution 194/III of 1948, which declares that "refugees wishing to return to their homes and live at peace with their neighbors should be permitted to do so at the earliest practicable date, and that compensation should be paid for property of those choosing not to return."

Natural increase of the 1948 refugee population, coupled with a new influx of homeless people after the June war, have raised the total of Palestinian refugees

---

[7] United Press International, dateline Jerusalem, May 5, 1969.
[8] Raymond H. Anderson, *New York Times,* April 25, 1969.
[9] *Ibid.,* April 23, 1969.
[10] Reuters, dateline Tel Aviv, May 12, 1969.

living in other Arab lands to well over one million. Close to 800,000 refugees are in Jordan, including many who still live in UNRWA-supported camps on the Israeli-occupied West Bank. Slightly more than 300,000 refugees remain in Gaza. (The Israeli government, by offering free transport and other inducements, persuaded nearly 40,000 Gazans to move to the East Bank of Jordan. In July 1968 the Jordanian government closed the Jordan River bridges to this traffic, charging that Israel was trying to empty Gaza at Jordan's expense.)[11]

Lebanon's refugee population numbers about 165,000, of whom slightly more than half live in camps and the rest on the economy. Syria plays host to some 248,000 Palestine refugees, of whom the bulk do not live in camps. Iraq never has accepted more than a few thousand refugees with special skills, though Iraq's rich river valley potentially could absorb many thousands of people.

A study conducted by two sociologists of the American University of Beirut in 1968 indicated that most refugees still wished to return to Palestine. Professors Peter Dodd and Halim Barakat interviewed 122 typical refugee families, comprising about 800 individuals, from many walks of life. Sixty-four percent of the 1948 refugees and 82 percent of people made homeless by the 1967 war declared they would go back. Only 15 percent of the old refugees and 2 percent of the new opted against return.[12]

Since the 1948 war Israel has taken back fewer than 100,000 refugees, under family reunion and other special categories. Israel refuses to accept more, on the grounds there is not enough room within the Jewish state and that Israel, by definition, must ingather its own people. The "law of return," adopted by the Knesset (Parliament) at the beginning of statehood, provides that "every Jew has a right to immigrate to Israel." In November 1961 the Knesset passed a resolution barring a mass return of Arab refugees to Israel and stating that the only solution to the problem was their settlement in Arab lands.

Israel charges, in part correctly, that some Arab governments deliberately have refused to integrate refugees, using their presence as a propaganda lever against Israel. In some cases there are special reasons for Arab reluctance. Lebanon has refused to give citizenship to its refugees, most of whom are Moslem, lest the nation's delicate Christian-Moslem balance be unhinged. Jordan gave citizenship to all refugees, but was unable to provide them jobs. Egypt offered to settle 50,000 refugees from Gaza in the Sinai Peninsula, if UNRWA engineers could find water. They could not and the plan was dropped. The Nile valley already was too crowded to take more people. Syria and Iraq are the most vulnerable to the charge of refugee neglect. Underpopulated and with cultivable land lying fallow, both countries have refused to absorb refugees, asserting that their settlement would imply the permanence of Israel.

Though Arab governments at first opposed the U.N. partition plan of 1947, they reconsidered their demands after the Arab-Israeli war of 1948 and insisted only on Israel's returning all lands *in excess* of the territory assigned to the Jewish state by the partition plan. This would have erased the conquests of the 1948 war,

---

[11] John K. Cooley, *The Christian Science Monitor,* April 30, 1969, p. 9.
[12] Cooley, *op. cit.,* p. 10.

when Israel increased its assigned territory by more than 30 percent. Israel, rejecting this demand, claimed the extra land was won in a war in which Jews were the victims, not the aggressors. Since the 1967 Mideast war, however, the Arabs have modified their demands and are now insisting only that Israel adhere to the principles of the November 22, 1967 United Nations Resolution which calls on Israel to return to its pre-1967 borders.

This list of topics indicates that the Arabs have reserve demands, particularly concerning refugees, which would remain to be solved, even if the results of the 1967 war could be nullified.

King Hussein, one of the most moderate—as well as beleaguered—Arab leaders, outlined a six-point Middle East peace plan in an address before the National Press Club in Washington in April 1969. Kernel of Hussein's plan, which he claimed was supported by President Nasser, was Arab readiness to recognize Israel and to grant the Jewish state freedom of navigation through the Suez Canal and Gulf of Aqaba. In return, Hussein declared, Israel must give up all territory it occupied during the 1967 war. This, the king stressed later on his return to Amman, included Jerusalem. The king described his plan as follows:

1. An end to all belligerency.
2. Respect for and acknowledgment of the sovereignty, territorial integrity, and political independence of all states in the area.
3. Recognition of the right of all Middle Eastern peoples to live within secure and recognized borders.
4. Guarantees of free navigation for all states through the Suez Canal and Gulf of Aqaba.
5. Guarantees of the territorial inviolability of all states in the area, through whatever measures were necessary, including the establishment of demilitarized zones.
6. A just settlement of the refugee problem.

The king's initiative, as will be seen, was rejected both by Israeli and by important segments of Arab opinion. Nonetheless, Hussein's six-point package—presented at a time of growing Arab-Israeli bitterness—carried the ring of compromise and courage.

Israeli Peace Conditions

On May 5, 1969, Prime Minister Golda Meir outlined Israel's conditions for making peace with the Arabs. "Peace," Mrs. Meir told the Knesset in Jerusalem, "must be expressed in signed peace treaties between Israel and each of the neighboring states. . . . The governments of the regions, and not external factors, are responsible for working out and drafting the peace treaties." [13] This reflected Israeli concern that the Big Four powers might impose a settlement on the Middle East, subject to later repudiation by the Arabs.

Any settlement acceptable to Moscow, the Israelis reasoned, necessarily would be detrimental to the Jewish state.

"The peace treaties," continued the prime minister, "must include agreement on agreed, secure, and recognized boundaries." This implied final Arab-Jewish fron-

---

[13] James Feron, *New York Times,* May 5, 1969.

38

tiers somewhere between the armistice lines of 1949 and the cease-fire lines of 1967. Mrs. Meir did not spell out what Israeli withdrawals might be made.

"The peace treaties," she went on, "must annul claims of belligerency, block-ades, boycotts, interference with free navigation and the existence and activity of organizations or groups engaged in preparing or executing sabotage operations from bases and training camps on the territories of the states signatory to the peace treaties." Much was included here, beyond abolition of the commando movement.

Israel was asking Egypt, as part of a peace package, to allow Israeli ships to transit the Suez Canal and the Strait of Tiran. This right had been sanctioned by the U.N. resolution of November 1967. But this problem, according to the semi-official Cairo newspaper *Al Ahram,* bore "no relation to the 1967 war or the liqui-dation of its consequences." [14] *Al Ahram* recalled statements by President Nasser, linking Israeli passage through the canal to settlement of the Palestine refugee problem. The newspaper also noted that the November 1967 resolution had referred only to "freedom of navigation in international waterways."[15] Egyptian officials claimed in May 1967 that both the Suez Canal and the Strait of Tiran were within Egyptian territorial waters.

Mrs. Meir also was pleading for an end to the Arab economic boycott of Israel. This boycott, instituted by the Arab League and administered from Damascus, seeks to prevent any Arab commerce with Israel and also to discourage foreign firms from trading with the Jewish state. Faced with loss of their trade with the Arab world, dozens of Western firms have complied with the boycott and severed commercial ties with Israel.

"No state will sign a treaty," Mrs. Meir concluded in her Knesset address, "with any other state aimed against its neighbor which is a co-signatory to the peace treaty." This appeared to mean that Israel anticipated, as part of a peace agree-ment, an end to inter-Arab pacts directed against the Jewish state.

U.S. Peace Initiative of June 1970

On June 19, 1970, the United States, backed by the Soviet Union, Britain, and France, proposed a peace initiative for the Middle East. It provided for a 90-day Arab-Israeli military standstill in the Suez Canal area and a general cease-fire, during which indirect talks between representatives of the hostile countries were to be conducted through the United Nations mediator, Dr. Gunnar V. Jarring. The talks would seek agreement on the establishment of peace in the Middle East, the basis of which was to be the United Nations Security Council Resolution of November 22, 1967.

On July 23 and 26, respectively, the United Arab Republic and Jordan an-nounced their willingness to cooperate in the peace initiative. Israel, on the other hand, fearful that Egypt would take advantage of the cease-fire to build up its Soviet-supplied missile strength along the Suez Canal, did not confirm her accept-ance of the plan until August 4.

---

[14] Raymond H. Anderson, *New York Times,* April 13, 1969.
[15] *Ibid.*

Once the agreement to seek peaceful solutions was announced, public protest arose in many parts of the Middle East. Egypt and Jordan were assailed by Syria, Iraq, Algeria, and, most vehemently, by the Palestinian commando groups as traitors to the Arab cause. Israel's agreement to the initiative prompted its right-wing Gahal faction to withdraw from Premier Meir's cabinet. Nevertheless, hope was mounting throughout the rest of the world that peace might be possible in the Middle East.

These hopes were disappointed, however, when, on September 7, Israel announced that she was withdrawing from the peace talks. Her Ambassador had met only once with U. N. Mediator Jarring. Israel's decision followed its repeated accusations that Egypt was deploying surface-to-air missile (SAM) batteries inside the Suez Canal cease-fire zone, a violation of the standstill agreement. Forward movement of the missiles, Israel claimed, was shifting the military balance in the canal zone to the advantage of Egypt. The United States delayed substantiating Israel's allegations at first, but later announced verification of the Soviet-Egyptian violations and called upon the Soviet Union and Egypt to "rectify" the situation.

An unexpected reaction to the peace initiative was the hijacking of four West European and American commercial airplanes with over 600 passengers aboard and the attempted hijacking of an Israeli commercial plane all within a period of four days in early September 1970. All hijackings were engineered by one Palestinian commando group, the Marxist Popular Front for the Liberation of Palestine, who were fearful that peace talks would doom the Palestinians' hopes to establish their own homeland in lands held by Israel. Eager to call attention to the existence and plight of the Palestinian people, PFLP ignored the hue and cry of world opinion against its dramatic and ruthless acts and claimed that commercial plane piracy was a legitimate war tactic, since the planes belonged to countries which espoused Zionism and were, therefore, enemies of the Palestinians. Also, in expressing its contempt for the Arab countries which joined the peace talks, the PFLP landed the hijacked planes on airstrips in Egypt and Jordan, an act meant to embarrass Nasser and Hussein. In further defiance of world opinion, the PFLP emptied the planes of all passengers and then blew up the planes, valued at approximately $50 million. Almost all the Arab nations, along with the other ten Palestinian guerrilla groups, joined the rest of the world in condemning the PFLP for terrorizing citizens and destroying property of countries not directly involved. The PFLP was suspended from the Unified Command of Palestine Resistance (UCPR), the association representing all the Palestinian commando groups.

The PFLP initially had announced that all passengers on the hijacked planes would be detained as hostages until nations holding Palestinian guerrillas allowed them to return to the Arab world. Although some American Jews and many holding Israeli passports were detained longer, eventually, however, all of the passengers were released.

Israel and Individual Arab States

Far from being monolithic, Israel's attitude toward the Arabs differs country by country. The "external" Arab lands—the Maghreb states of North Africa, Libya, the Sudan, Saudi Arabia, and the Persian Gulf sheikdoms—have in the past had little continuing involvement, beyond verbal, in the Palestine problem. The leftist government in the Sudan has stressed hostility to Israel, but it is unclear what concrete measures Khartoum might adopt. Attitude of Libya's new revolutionary regime to the Palestine problem will be discussed in connection with French policy toward the Middle East. President Bourguiba's Tunisia, the most relaxed of all Arab nations toward the Jewish state, has allowed limited mail and travel contact between Israelis and Tunisian citizens. I recall the surprise I felt on being able to buy Israeli stamps freely at a philatelist's shop in Tunis. Kuwait, Saudi Arabia, and Libya—the oil-rich states—display a brand of Arab solidarity, by paying subsidies to Egypt and Jordan to compensate for their economic losses in 1967.

Iraq

Iraq, also external in the sense of having no common frontier with Israel, is more directly involved. Iraqi army units are stationed in Jordan and successive governments in Baghdad have expressed strong anti-Zionism. In 1969 the Iraqi government aroused Israeli anger by hanging nine Iraqi Jews as Israeli spies. Through third parties, Israel tried to obtain the emigration of the 2,500 to 3,000 Jews estimated to be left in Iraq, remnant of the once-flourishing Jewish community which owed its origin to the Assyrian and Babylonian conquests of the pre-Christian era. In January 1970 Golda Meir told the Knesset in Jerusalem that Iraqi officials appeared to be holding their Jewish community hostage, in the apparent hope that Israel would moderate military attacks on Iraqi forces.

Lebanon

Of the Arab states which share frontiers with Israel, three—Lebanon, Syria, and Jordan—pose no fundamental threat to Israeli security. The Lebanese government does its best to keep at arms length from the Palestine dispute. During the early 1960s the Lebanese air force stayed prudently on the ground, while Israeli jets flew high-level patrols up Lebanon's Bekaa Valley, plotting the passes leading through the Anti-Lebanon Mountains to Damascus. The commander of Lebanon's armed forces vetoed Lebanese participation in the 1967 war.

All this reflects the delicate internal situation of Lebanon, a nation of roughly 2,600,000 people—smaller in size and population than Israel. An official French census in 1932, during the French mandate in Lebanon, found the country to have a 55 to 45 percent Christian-Moslem relationship. This allowed the French to give a controlling position to Lebanese Christians, who, by tradition, supply the president of the nation, while Sunni Moslems provide the prime minister. Not since the French departed has the Lebanese government conducted a census, for fear it would disclose what the Moslems claim—that the higher Moslem birth rate has reversed the percentages.

Many Christian Lebanese, including highly prosperous businessmen, want peace with the Zionist state, partly for the Lebanese-Israeli trade which peace would permit, even more to remove a dangerous irritant from Lebanese national life.

Moslem Lebanese, including the country's restive Palestinian refugees, share general Arab bitterness toward Israel.

Lately the Syrians, who never have been reconciled to the loss of Lebanon since the French separated the rich coastal plain from the Syrian hinterland, have sent units of al-Saiqa—the Syrian branch of the commando movement—into southern Lebanon. The ostensible reason is to launch guerrilla attacks on Israel from Lebanese bases. But the Syrians may be equally interested in stirring Lebanese Moslems to revolt against the Christian-dominated social structure, with the hope of absorbing Lebanon within a Greater Syria.

Al-Saiqa raids into Israel from Lebanon drew a punishing Israeli reprisal on Lebanese civil aircraft at Beirut Airport in December 1968. At the beginning of 1970 Arab guerrillas raided the Israeli village of Metullah and seized an Israeli guard. Israeli forces stormed back across the border into Lebanon and captured 22 Lebanese.

This incident was preceded by a brief civil war between the Lebanese army and Arab guerrilla detachments. An uneasy modus vivendi finally was hammered out between Lebanese authorities and the commandos, partly through Egyptian mediation. The Lebanese government agreed to allow al-Saiqa and al-Fatah units to remain on Lebanese soil. In fact the government had little choice, for an effort to oust the guerrillas would have aroused fundamental Moslem opposition. In return the guerrillas promised not to shoot across the border into Israel from Lebanon. They said they would not set up their camps closer than 500 to 1,000 yards from any Lebanese town. Finally, military training of commandos no longer would be conducted within Lebanon's Palestine refugee camps. In an effort to enforce the agreement the Lebanese government removed Maj. Gen. Emile Bustani as commander-in-chief of the army and replaced him with Maj. Gen. Jean Njaim, generally regarded as a tougher man.

The government's efforts to insulate Lebanese national life from the Palestine problem, showed how vulnerable is Lebanon's unique Christian-Moslem partnership to outside pressures. An ironic remark attributed to former Israeli Foreign Minister Moshe Sharett remains accurate. He did not know, Sharett declared, which Arab state would be the first to make peace with Israel. But Lebanon would be the second.

Syria

Syrians, like Iraqis, are deeply hostile to Israel. The Syrian government signed an armistice with Israel in 1949, which Iraq refused to do. But a succession of weak Syrian governments has used the struggle to liberate Palestine as a rallying cry to win popular support. Meanwhile, about 4,000 Jews remaining in Syria lead a tense existence in Damascus, Aleppo, and the smaller town of Kemishli.

Syrian artillery on the Golan Heights periodically fired on neighboring Israeli kibbutzim and made life miserable for Jewish fishing boats in waters which Syria considered to be in the demilitarized zone. Now Syria no longer has the Golan Heights and is unable to strike effectively at Israel, except through indirect encouragement of guerrilla forces. Kibbutz Golan was the first of several Israeli villages established on the former Syrian heights.

At one time the complex problem of sharing Jordan River waters caused a crisis between Syria and Israel. The latter, to bring water to its barren Negev, began work in 1953 on a water diversion canal at the B'not Yaakov bridge on the Jordan River, between Lake Huleh and the Sea of Galilee. This work fell within a demilitarized zone established between Israel and Syria. Damascus obtained a United Nations stop work order against Israel, which was reinforced by the cutting off of American aid to the Jewish state, until Israeli technicians left the B'not Yaakov site.

Israeli engineers then switched their link-up point south from B'not Yaakov to a place just north of the Sea of Galilee and wholly within Israel. At the same time work was progressing on a 108-inch pipeline to channel the water south to the parched Negev. Meanwhile, the Arab riparian states complained that diversion of the Jordan River by Israel would deprive Lebanon, Syria, and Jordan of their rightful share. A formula worked out by Eric Johnston, special envoy of President Eisenhower, allocated 60 percent of Jordan River waters to the three Arab states affected and 40 percent to Israel. This meant 400 million cubic meters for the Jewish state.

Israeli engineers accepted the plan, though Israel's original demand had been for 550 million cubic meters. Arab engineers also favored the Johnston plan, but were overruled by their governments. As the issue hung fire year after year at the United Nations, Israel completed its diversion works, including a reservoir at Sahl Batouf, near Nazareth. In 1959 the Israeli government expressed alarm at the rate the nation's water table was falling from overuse. No international problem remained, in the Israeli view, since the planned diversion would take place wholly within Israeli territory and the Zionists would take only the amount of water awarded to them by the Johnston plan. The taps were turned and water from the Sea of Galilee now gushes through the huge pipeline to the Negev desert, prime settlement land for new immigrants to Israel.

Jordan

King Hussein's urgent need to regain the West Bank already has been described. In the summer of 1967, when the shock of defeat still was fresh, a number of West Bank leaders spoke out for the establishment of some kind of Palestine entity, linked politically to Jordan and economically to Israel. These Palestinians were ready to accept cooperation with Israel, provided they were backed up by Jordan's king. Hussein put out feelers for American support and was disappointed. He tried next, also in vain, to win permission from other Arab kings and presidents for Jordan to go it alone with Israel.

Meanwhile, the recruitment and training of guerrillas by al-Fatah in Jordan had aroused public admiration and expectations. King Hussein's freedom of maneuver, limited at best, was dwindling to nothing. He made a final appeal to President Nasser. Would the president help Hussein stay in power and pacify his people, if Jordan made a separate peace with Israel? Nasser's reply, according to excellent diplomatic sources, was in three parts:

1. Hussein could do as he wished with the West Bank, which belonged to Jordan alone.

2. Nasser could not, or would not, help Hussein keep the guerrillas in check.

3. Jerusalem belonged, not only to Jordan, but to all Arabs. Hussein would not be allowed to make a separate deal with the Jews on Jerusalem.

Thus rebuffed, King Hussein went to Washington in April 1969 and gained an option to buy a second squadron of F-104 jet interceptors, plus other military equipment, from the United States. Delivery of a first squadron began during the summer of 1969. Washington also signed an agreement under which Jordan would receive 735,000 bushels of American wheat on long-term credit. These concessions were designed to demonstrate American backing of Hussein, though not to the point of guaranteeing his throne.

Hussein, as we have seen, also used his Washington trip to launch a peace proposal in a speech before the National Press Club. Hussein's six-point plan was denounced by al-Fatah and by the governments of Algeria, Iraq, and Saudi Arabia, who claimed to see in it a plot to abandon the Arab struggle for Palestine. President Nasser, in whose name Hussein also had claimed to speak, failed to support the King explicitly. All this led *al-Jarida*, a Beirut daily newspaper, to write: "The Arabs have let Hussein down." Saudi Arabia hinted at the end of its post-1967 subsidy to Jordan, if King Hussein persisted in seeking a compromise peace.

The king's initiative also was rejected by Israel, on the grounds it contained nothing new and ignored the necessity for direct Arab-Jewish negotiations. "If, having decided to make war in June 1967, you have now decided to make peace, then come to the negotiating table." [16] So Israeli Foreign Minister Abba Eban addressed himself to King Hussein.

"We do not wish to push the Israelis into the sea," declared a Jordanian official privately. "But they have pushed us into the desert. Believe me, the desert is worse than the sea. In the water you die in a few minutes. In the desert it takes days." In the long run, this official believed, Jordan had no choice but to make peace with the Jewish state. "What else," he asked, "can we do?"

Logically the Jordanian official may have been right. Yet King Hussein's political options narrowed even more in June 1970, when a short-lived civil war between Arab guerrillas and the Jordanian army killed or wounded nearly 1,000 persons in Amman. The fighting left the Popular Front for the Liberation of Palestine (PFLP)—the main commando group involved in the fighting—in effective control of much of Amman. Hussein was forced to yield to PFLP demands, including the firing of his uncle, Maj. Gen. Sherif Nasser Ben Jamil, as army commander in chief. The king also halted army shelling of the PFLP stronghold in the Wahdat refugee camp near Amman.

Later King Hussein and Palestinian leaders agreed on a 16-point peace plan, whose effect was to turn the Jordanian capital into a neutral city. The government pledged to withdraw army units from Amman. The commandos promised to take most of their armed men out of the capital. Four Arab mediating nations—Egypt, Sudan, Libya, and Algeria—guaranteed freedom of movement and action for guerrilla forces throughout the rest of Jordan. This compromise disappeared in the virtual war which broke out between the commandos and the Jordanian army in September 1970.

---

[16] Reuters, dateline Jerusalem, April 13, 1969.

In effect the major commando groups now share power in the Hashemite kingdom with Hussein and his government. But this crisis, while strengthening the commando position overall, did expose differences and possible tension between Yasser Arafat, commander of al-Fatah, and George Habbash, Christian leader of the PFLP.

Egypt

Israelis regard the United Arab Republic as their chief adversary. The most populous Arab land, with the largest and best-equipped armed forces, Egypt is in a position at any time to inflict a dangerous blow on Israel, at least from the air. But Egypt also is vulnerable. Well-placed Israeli bombs might destroy or damage the giant Aswan Dam, releasing the pent-up waters of the Nile to cascade down the valley, wreaking havoc on the peasants of the Nile. Nonetheless, Israel cannot rule out a pre-emptive strike by the only Arab air force equipped to deliver one.

Israeli and American specialists disagree on the extent to which the Soviets rearmed the Egyptians after 1967. Late in 1969 Israeli Defense Minister Moshe Dayan was quoted as saying that Egypt had 70 percent more weapons than before the 1967 war and that Syria, Iraq, and Jordan each had 50 percent more. American experts, having reexamined their information in the light of the Dayan statement, gave out the estimate that the Soviets had replaced 100 percent of Arab losses, but not more. This was said to be an average, with some lines of equipment a bit more, others a bit less.

Quality of the new Egyptian arsenal was thought to be superior to pre-1967. The Egyptian air force, according to intelligence experts, now has about 90 Sukhoi-7 fighter planes, against very few of this advanced model before the 1967 hostilities. This upgrading, American officials pointed out, was countered by Israel's acquisition of 50 F-4 Phantoms from the United States.

In September 1969 the Egyptian air force was authoritatively described as consisting of 400 combat aircraft, broken down as follows—12 TU-16 medium jet bombers; 30 IL-28 light jet bombers; 100 MIG-21 jet interceptors; 90 SU-7 fighter-bombers; 120 MIG-15 and MIG-17 fighter-bombers, plus transport planes, helicopters, and jet trainers. Air defense was provided by a wide variety of antiaircraft guns, and by 300 SAM-2 surface-to-air missiles deployed in 30 batteries of six launchers each. Later estimates pinpointed the emplacement of SAM-3 missile batteries, designed to operate against low-flying Israeli aircraft. A separate Egyptian Missile Command, employing 4,000 men, was thought to dispose of about 100 Egyptian-built ground-to-ground missiles.[17]

Israeli forces claim to have destroyed 64 Egyptian planes between the end of the 1967 war and the beginning of 1970. Even more damaging to Egypt than the loss of planes is the nature of the deeply-penetrating raids which the Israeli army and air force have been conducting. A spectacular example was the seizure by Israeli forces in December 1969 of a complete Soviet-built radar system from the Red Sea coast of Egypt. This was described by Maj. Gen. Haim Herzog, former chief of Israeli army intelligence, as a P-12 type, the first of its kind to fall intact into Western hands.

---

[17] *The Military Balance 1969–1970* (London: The Institute for Strategic Studies), p. 37.

This raid was followed by the Israeli seizure of the Red Sea island of Shadwan, a key point in the Egyptian radar monitoring network. Israeli troops destroyed Egyptian installations on the island, killed an estimated 70 Egyptian soldiers, captured many more, and took away with them a British-made marine-surveillance radar station. This type of land raid was supplemented by frequent bombings of Egyptian industrial and military targets by Israeli aircraft.

On January 28, 1970, General Dayan described these land and air actions as having a threefold purpose—to relieve pressure on Israeli troops along the Suez Canal; to prevent any Egyptian move to open full-scale war; and to convince the Egyptian people that its leadership was unable to provide the nation with adequate defense.

Disclosure that Soviet experts themselves were manning some SAM missile sites in Egypt disturbed the Israelis, but apparently did not change their basic strategy. Chaim Bar-Lev, Israeli army chief of staff, declared his nation's readiness to fight Soviet forces, should the latter try to drive Israeli troops out of their positions east of the Suez Canal.

Israeli officials noted that Egypt, apart from immediate equipment needs, was peculiarly dependent on the USSR to wage a long war—much more so than Israel depended on outside powers. "A MIG engine cannot be overhauled in Egypt," affirmed an Israeli official. "It must be sent back to the Soviet Union. So must a tank engine for a complete overhaul."

The Soviet Union gave no indication of wanting a new Arab-Jewish war at this stage. Nor would the Egyptian army be ready for months to launch a campaign, even if Nasser were ready to risk lack of matériel support from Moscow. What then were Cairo's intentions?

Israeli leaders distrusted President Nasser's expressed readiness, in interviews with Western newsmen, to accept the "reality" of Israel, given a solution to all pending problems. Israelis believed that Nasser felt he had a fair chance of bringing enough international pressure on Israel for the latter to withdraw from Sinai, without Egypt having to give up anything vital. Permission for Israel to use the Suez Canal, for example, could be withdrawn, once Israeli troops were safely out of Sinai. The Jews would have lost their leverage to open the canal to Israeli vessels, short of launching a new military drive across the desert. World opinion would not accept this, the Israelis thought.

They intended, therefore, to stay where they were, at least until President Nasser agreed to sit down, face to face, with the prime minister of Israel and sign a peace treaty. Meanwhile, Israel resisted in every way possible any substitute Big Four solution, which would excuse Mr. Nasser from the painful task of talking with the Jews.

Following the abortive Arab summit conference at Rabat in December 1969, Nasser appeared to be contemplating an alliance of Egypt, Libya, and the Sudan —the latter two nations now having military leaders sympathetic to him. The Arab summit had failed to back up Mr. Nasser with concrete promises of men and money with which to combat Israel. The Egyptian leader flew directly from Rabat to Tripoli, Libya, for talks with Libyan and Sudanese leaders. These centered on the feasibility of a Northeast African alliance, which Gen. Gafaar al-Numeiry of Sudan called "natural, logical, and inevitable." The conferees were said by Tripoli radio to have explored, not only a military grouping, but an agricultural credit bank, common trade policies, and a combined airline.

Arab Commandos

Anyone who, over the years, visited the Palestine refugees in their miserable camps should not have been surprised at the rise of the guerrilla movement. Participating in al-Fatah, the Palestine Liberation Organization, or another of the commando groups gives a young Palestinian not only the conviction that he is fighting for his homeland, but a sense of purpose, a release from apathy and frustration.

From the moment of implementation of the terms set forth in the Balfour Declaration until the creation of the State of Israel in 1947, the major conflict in the Middle East was one between Palestinian Arabs and Zionist Jews in Palestine. Once Israel was established as a state, however, the issue became diffused into an Arab-Israeli conflict when the other Arab nations adopted the Palestinian issue as their own. When the 1967 war proved again that regular Arab armies were no match for Israel's armed forces, the hour of the Palestinian commandos came. They decided they had to take matters into their own hands, if effective blows were to be struck against the Zionist state: "the conflict is between Israelis and Palestinians, not Israelis and Arabs." [18] The process had gone full cycle and once again the Palestinians were conspicuous contenders in the battle for their "homeland."

The commandos at first enjoyed little favor among Arab governments. On June 26, 1962, President Nasser told refugee representatives from Gaza: "I do not agree with becoming involved in semimilitary operations. If we are engaged in such operations how could we guarantee that Ben-Gurion would (not) also be engaged in semimilitary operations?" [19] Mr. Nasser's attitude, shared by Jordanian and Lebanese leaders, was that commando operations invited Israeli reprisals, with which organized Arab armies could not cope. Also, powerful groups of armed refugees threatened to become states within states.

Following the debacle of June 1967, discredited Arab leaders could do little but swim with the rising tide of commando militancy. Jordan now openly allows al-Fatah to operate from the Hashemite Kingdom, though King Hussein tries to keep the guerrillas within prescribed bounds. "People often say," remarked a senior Israeli diplomat, "that Hussein is a moderate Arab, with whom we could deal. Perhaps so. Certainly he is better than those Baath leaders in Baghdad or Damascus. But we Israelis cannot forget that Hussein attacked us in 1967 and that he permits al-Fatah to assault us from Jordan."

Nasser also has gone over to support of the commando cause. In May 1969

---

[18] (Words spoken by Abu Amar in an interview with an NBC television reporter), Paul A. Jureidini, *The Palestinian Revolution: Its Organizations, Ideologies, and Dynamics* (Washington, D. C.: The American University, Center for Research in Social Systems, May 1970), p. 30.

[19] Y. Harkabi, *Fedayeen Action and Arab Strategy* (London: The Institute for Strategic Studies, Adelphi Papers Number Fifty-Three, December 1968), p. 5. This study describes the rise of the commando movement, its organization, philosophy, and goals.

Mohammed Hassanein Heikal, editor of the Cairo newspaper *Al Ahram* and a confidant of President Nasser, called on multifarious Palestinian factions to unite, along the lines of the National Liberation Front in South Vietnam.[20] "The struggle inside occupied Palestinian territory," Heikal said, "must be carried on under the Palestinian flag, raised only by an organization capable of assimilating all the forces of the popular armed struggle for Palestine." Heikal cited al-Fatah as such a group.

The Iraqi government, by contrast, ordered guerrilla leaders to subject themselves to Iraqi control, to stop uniformed commandos from entering Iraqi towns, and to remove guerrilla training centers from urban areas. Finally, the Baghdad regime set up a rival commando group called the Arab Front for the Liberation of Palestine, apparently to undercut the growing popularity of al-Fatah. Syria supports its own commando splinter group, al-Saiqa, while the Lebanese government battles to keep the various commando factions under Lebanese army control.

At least two Soviet journals have published criticism of al-Fatah's refusal to accept a political settlement of the Palestine dispute. Moscow, willing to settle for something less than the destruction of Israel, apparently feels the commandos threaten to undermine the Arab regimes through which the Soviet Union works in the Middle East.

More than ten commando groups were operating from neighboring territories against Israel in the summer of 1970.

The most significant commando organization is al-Fatah. Founded in 1965 by Yasser Arafat, alias Abu Ammar, al-Fatah rejects any peaceful settlement in the Middle East and proclaims armed struggle to be the only way to regain "our Palestine" and to replace the Zionist state with a non-theocratic state of both Palestinians and Jews.[21] Arafat, a Palestinian who was forced to flee from Egypt in 1954 because of his affiliation with the Moslem Brotherhood, has become the dominant commando figure and a popular hero to countless Arabs, who once looked to Gamal Abdel Nasser for inspiration.

Al-Fatah contends that the liberation of Palestine must precede Arab unity, instead of the other way around. Nasser used to argue that, until the Arabs were united, they had little hope of defeating Israel. Arafat describes the "Zionist existence" as "the root of all (Arab) diseases and not one of their consequences." [22] Hence the Zionist state must be eradicated, before the Arabs can unite and reform their social and political structures. From this follows al-Fatah's refusal to entertain halfway solutions.

In 1964 Arab governments created the Palestine Liberation Organization (PLO), as the only official body authorized to speak for Palestinians. The PLO has a 7,000-man Palestine Liberation Army (PLA), based mainly in Syria, Egypt, and Iraq. Under the leadership of Ahmed Shukairy, the PLO, like Arab governments, was tarred by the brush of defeat in June 1967. In February 1969 Yasser Arafat swept aside the old leadership and became chairman of the 11-man executive committee of the PLO.

---

[20] Anderson, *op. cit.,* May 9, 1969.
[21] Jureidini, *op. cit.,* p. 31.
[22] Harkabi, *op. cit.,* p. 8.

Two months later Arafat announced formation of a Palestinian Armed Struggle Command (PASC), comprising the military forces of al-Fatah, the PLA, al-Saiqa, and most other guerrilla groups. The purpose of PASC was merely to improve cooperation in the military field. Nevertheless, the Marxist Popular Front for the Liberation of Palestine refused to join PASC for ideological reasons. In February 1970, yet another organization, the Unified Command of Palestine Resistance (UCPR), was created. More neutral in ideology, its membership included all guerrilla groups.

Al-Fatah claims to have killed at least 1,200 Israeli soldiers since 1965, at a price of 308 dead Arab guerrillas.[23] This figure of Israelis killed by commandos is rejected by Jewish officials. Yehuda Miron of the Israeli Defense Ministry declared on June 8, 1969, that shelling, sniping, and guerrilla attacks altogether had killed 669 Israeli soldiers from the end of the June war through April 1969. This compared with 780 Jewish soldiers killed during the six-day war itself.

In any event, the military effectiveness of commandos is not the major concern. The real problem, from the standpoint of Israel, moderate Arabs, and outside powers alike, is the relative ability of the commando movement to sabotage an eventual peace settlement, by weakening public support of the Arab governments which might agree to end the war. Awareness of this problem became even more acute after the PFLP hijacked four jet airplanes in September 1970—an act designed to subvert the already-delicate Arab-Israeli cease-fire negotiations.

---

[23] Eric Pace, *New York Times,* January, 12, 1969..

V. UNITED STATES AND ISRAEL

In the spring of 1969 a paid advertisement, signed by 59 United States senators and 238 representatives, appeared in a number of American newspapers. This ad, placed by the American Israel Public Affairs Committee, Inc., was headlined: "A Declaration . . . in favor of Direct Arab-Israel Peace Negotiations, on the occasion of Israel's 21st birthday, April 23rd, 1969, Endorsed by a majority of the Senate and House of Representatives."

The words of the advertisement purported to be those of the American legislators who signed. After congratulating Israelis on their two decades of progress, the legislators expressed their "concern that the people of Israel are still denied their right to peace and that they must carry heavy defense burdens which divert human and material resources from productive pursuits."

"We deeply regret," the Declaration continued, "that Israel's Arab neighbors, after three futile and costly wars, still refuse to negotiate a final peace settlement with Israel. We believe that the issues which divide Israel and the Arab states can be resolved in the spirit and service of peace, if the leaders of the Arab states would agree to meet with Israelis in face-to-face negotiations. There is no effective substitute for the procedure. . . . We oppose any attempt by outside powers to impose halfway measures not conducive to a permanent peace."

This last sentence is significant. At the moment these legislators put their names to this document, President Nixon's Administration was searching for a Big Four solution to the Middle East impasse with the Soviet Union, Britain, and France. Israel objects to this approach. More than half the elected representatives of the American people were saying, in effect, that they disagreed with United States government policy and agreed with Israel.

Few, if any, other foreign governments could persuade a majority of American congressmen to sign a statement at variance with United States policy. True, it was not the government of Israel which placed the ad. But every word of the Declaration might have been written in Jerusalem and certainly would have been welcomed there. Signers included senators of such disparate views as Barry Goldwater, Edward M. Kennedy, George Murphy, Edward W. Brooke, Ralph W.

Yarborough, and Charles H. Percy. It would be hard to find another controversial issue on which this mixed bag of conservatives and liberals, Republicans and Democrats, could agree.

For more than 20 years, from President Truman's instant recognition of Israel in 1948 to the placing of the Israel Public Affairs Committee ad in 1969, the Palestine problem has been intimately involved in domestic American politics. Early evidence of the political content of U.S. government policy on the issue was disclosed by Col. William A. Eddy, United States Minister to Saudi Arabia from 1944-46. Writing after his retirement, Colonel Eddy told of the recall to Washington in 1946 of four American diplomats stationed in the Middle East—the American Ministers to Egypt, Lebanon and Syria (a joint post), Saudi Arabia, and the Consul General to mandated Palestine.

President Truman asked for the diplomats' views on the effects of American policy in Palestine. The substance of what the diplomats said was that American relations with the Arabs would be gravely jeopardized by one-sided partiality to the Zionists. "Mr. Truman," wrote Colonel Eddy, "summed up his position with the utmost candor: 'I'm sorry, gentlemen, but I have to answer to hundreds of thousands who are anxious for the success of Zionism: I do not have hundreds of thousands of Arabs among my constituents.' " [1]

Mr. Truman's decision to work for the creation of Israel ran directly counter to the advice of American diplomats in the area. The latter felt it was not a question of being "pro-Arab" or "anti-Jewish." The fact was that support of Israel would cause damage to wider American interests in the Middle East. "If our government in Washington decides it wants to side with Israel," declared an American diplomat privately, "it is not our business as Ambassadors to Middle Eastern countries to object. But it is our job to point out very clearly what will be the costs involved." [2]

American Interests in the Middle East

The wider American interests referred to included access to Arab oil and denial of the Middle East to the Communists. Oil from the Middle East is important to the United States, but vital to America's allies in Western Europe and to Japan. The United States, from its own reserves and those in South America, could get along without Arab oil. But Britain, France, West Germany, and other European powers could not. Seventy-six percent of Western Europe's oil imports come from the Middle East and North Africa. Japan gets 85 percent of its petroleum imports from these sources. Loss of access to Middle Eastern oil would force the United States to deplete its own and Latin American reserves to keep Western Europe supplied.

The United States also depends on Arab oil to supply its military installations around the world, ranging in a long arc from Iceland, down through Europe and the Mediterranean, to the Far East. NATO components, including the U.S. Sixth Fleet in the Mediterranean, depend on Middle Eastern oil. So do the U.S. Seventh

---

[1] William A. Eddy, *F.D.R. Meets Ibn Saud* (New York: American Friends of the Middle East, Inc., 1954), pp. 36–37.

[2] Ellis, *Challenge in the Middle East, op. cit.,* p. 93.

Fleet in the Pacific and, to a great extent, the American military machine in Vietnam.

Domination of the Middle East by the Soviet Union would jeopardize Western access to Arab oil. The Soviets, oil exporters themselves, do not need petroleum from the Middle East, though forecasts indicate that in time the Soviets may become net petroleum importers. In any event, the ability to deny Arab oil to the West would shift the world's strategic balance in favor of the Communists. Soviet control of the Middle East also would cut American and Western defense links with South Asia and the Far East. These factors, in the view of State Department experts, dictated a policy of American friendship with the Arabs.

President Truman decided otherwise, with the result that almost overnight the United States—the power almost universally admired by Arabs in the days of Woodrow Wilson—became Arab enemy number one. Withdrawal of British and French influence from the Middle East after World War II created a power vacuum which the United States and the Soviets jousted to fill. It might, in any case, have proven impossible to keep the Soviets out of the area, since the United States—simply to serve its Arab interests—could not have become anti-Israel. The desperate plight of European Jewry and the need to help the Jewish state absorb refugees from Europe aroused the American conscience.

Nonetheless, Arab hostility to Washington immensely complicated policymaking in the Middle East and directly contributed to Soviet penetration of the Arab world. Unburdened by conscience, the Soviets used the Palestine problem to curry Arab favor and, in the process, to make Egypt, Syria, and to some degree Iraq, dependent on Soviet arms.

By no means do the Soviets dominate the Middle East today. Nor have they blocked the flow of Arab oil to the West. Finally, having failed to go to President Nasser's rescue in 1967, the Soviets are having to step nimbly to retain Arab favor. Moscow has demonstrated that its support of the Arabs stops short of risking war with the United States. But the Soviets must be reckoned with as a permanent factor in the Middle East, ranged on the Arab side, while the United States is regarded by most Arabs as pro-Israel.

Having made a political decision to support the Zionists, the United States helped to sustain the new state in its formative years. In 1950 the United States joined Britain and France in issuing a Tripartite Declaration, guaranteeing the territorial integrity of Middle Eastern states. This had the effect of sanctioning Israel's 1948 wartime expansion beyond U.N. partition plan frontiers.

Israel's economy, as will be seen, is beset by a chronic imbalance of payments —an excess of imports over exports. A significant factor enabling the Jewish state to offset this deficit has been aid from the United States, official and unofficial.

Except in 1948 and 1951, Israel in its early years received more economic help from the United States government than did all Arab states combined. This situation prevailed until 1955, when the Arabs, taken together, received slightly more aid than Israel.

American assistance to Israel included outright grants, technical assistance, Development Loan Fund loans, surplus farm products under the Public Law 480 program, and loans from the Export-Import Bank. Only in 1959 did the Arab

53

states begin to get substantially more aid from the United States than Israel received.

The following table, in millions of dollars, compares official American help to Israel and to Arab states combined during the first 12 years of the Jewish state's existence. The Arab countries lumped together include Egypt, Iraq, Jordan, Lebanon, Saudi Arabia, and the Sudan:

	U.S. Government Economic Aid to Israel since May 1948	U.S. Government Economic Aid to Arab states since May 1948
Fiscal year:		
1948	none	7.3
1949	none	none
1950	135.0	none
1951	none	4.8
1952	63.5	9.5
1953	73.7	20.1
1954	54.0	25.8
1955	54.6	56.2
1956	54.4	39.9
1957	37.5	37.68
1958	89.2	70.9
1959	52.4	114.5
Grand total:	$614,300,000	$386,480,000[3]

To this total must be added contributions to Israel from private American citizens. Consistently over the years American Jews have donated at least $60 million a year through the United Jewish Appeal and another $50 million through purchase of State of Israel bonds. During crisis years these and other contributions, including investments in Israeli enterprises, have risen steeply. Altogether, the United States government, from 1950 through 1967, gave or loaned nearly $1 billion to the Jewish state. During the same period world Jewry contributed more than $4.5 billion, much of this coming from American Jews.[4]

Eisenhower Policy Change

The first phase of United States policy—open partiality to Israel—ended with the election of President Eisenhower. The new President did not turn his back on the Jewish state, but sought rather to balance American initiatives in the Middle East. General Eisenhower's accession to the White House heralded a rise in American technical, economic, and financial aid to Arab governments. This tendency accelerated under President Kennedy, whose administration in 1963 gave Egypt about $220 million worth of help, principally in food. Jordan received $53 million in American assistance during the same year, against $80 million for Israel.

---

[3] Figures supplied by the United States government.
[4] Oded Remba, "The Dilemmas of Israel's Economy," *Midstream,* February 1969, p. 57.

After 1960 the United Arab Republic became the single largest recipient of United States aid in the Middle East, excluding Turkey and Iran, which lie somewhat outside the focus of the Palestine problem. Following the 1967 war Egypt and six other Arab states broke relations with Washington. Since then the United States has initiated no new aid programs to these countries.

President Eisenhower demonstrated American even-handedness in the Middle East in 1956, by applying effective pressure on Britain, France, and Israel to withdraw their forces from Egyptian territory. Earlier, however, American-Egyptian relations had suffered a decline, through Secretary of State Dulles' refusal to sell American arms to President Nasser. In February 1955 Israeli army units had attacked Egyptian positions in Gaza, killing 38 Egyptian soldiers. This was in reprisal for Arab guerrilla raids mounted from the Gaza Strip. An aroused Nasser, fearful of losing the support of his officer corps, appealed to Washington to sell him $100 million worth of weapons. Later he scaled down his request to about $20 million. He did not intend to use these weapons aggressively against Israel, the Egyptian leader argued. But he had to improve the morale of his troops and soothe unrest among Egyptian officers.

This dialogue took place against the backdrop of the Baghdad Pact, designed by the United States and British governments to erect a northern tier alliance of pro-Western Middle Eastern states. Nasser resented the pact as an encroachment on his concept of Egyptian and Arab "positive neutrality" and as an Anglo-American effort to strengthen anti-Nasser elements in Iraq and other Arab lands. Secretary Dulles, for his part, was convinced that Cairo's charismatic leader was striving to overthrow pro-Western governments in Lebanon, Jordan, and Iraq. In this atmosphere of mutual distrust the projected arms deal fell through.

The Soviet Union now entered the scene, offering massive quantities of arms to Nasser, to be paid for with Egyptian cotton. Moscow placed no restrictions on the use of these arms. Nasser informed the United States of the Soviet offer and renewed his plea for American military help. At this juncture George V. Allen, Assistant Secretary of State for Near Eastern and African Affairs, was dispatched from Washington, reportedly to deliver an "ultimatum" to Cairo. If Nasser accepted the Soviets' arms offer, Washington would retaliate with economic strictures.[5]

Nasser's answer was to deliver a speech, announcing the acceptance of Soviet weapons to strengthen Egyptian forces against Israel. To Dulles, Nasser had become the villain who had opened the Middle East to Soviet entry. In retaliation, Washington ended its CARE school lunch program for Egyptian children, barred the sale of lubricating oils to Egypt, and tried to deny Cairo access to spare parts for American machinery. The crowning blow was withdrawal of an American offer to help Egypt build the High Aswan Dam. Here, too, the Russians stepped into the breach, with the result that the Soviet Union gained credit for constructing Egypt's most monumental engineering project since the Pyramids.

President Nasser's angry response to the West was to nationalize the Suez Canal. When this in turn brought on the French-British-Israeli invasion of Egypt,

---

[5] For background on American-Egyptian negotiations during this period see Ellis, *Challenge in the Middle East, op. cit.,* chapter three.

55

Washington regained some favor in Cairo's eyes by forcing the invaders to retreat. Over succeeding years American relations with the United Arab Republic progressed from "attentive inactivity" to restoration of aid programs.[6] Several projects developed, including the resumption of CARE lunches to more than one million Egyptian children and the leasing of a giant U.S. army hopper dredge to improve the Suez Canal, at a price $1,600 per day less than an American firm would have had to pay.

Meanwhile, Israeli-Egyptian tension increased, as Soviet arms poured into the UAR arsenal and the Egyptians began to fortify the Sinai desert. Israel resented American aid to Cairo, which—as the Israelis saw it—released Egyptian resources to magnify their arms purchases from the Soviets. In 1963 Israeli Prime Minister Ben-Gurion demanded an American-Soviet guarantee of Israel's frontiers. Failing in this, the Israeli leader pressed for a mutual defense pact between Israel and the United States. His government, Ben-Gurion told the Knesset, had indisputable evidence that the Arabs were planning to attack the Jewish state.

President Kennedy rejected a mutual defense pact, but—according to official Israeli interpretation—pledged American support in the event of Arab aggression. Washington also sold the Jewish state a battalion of Hawk antiaircraft ground-to-air missiles, at a price of $25 million to offset Egypt's advantage in jet aircraft. (On May 21, 1969, an Egyptian MIG-21 was shot down over Sinai by a direct hit from a Hawk missile. "To the best of my knowledge," declared an Israeli spokesman, "[this was] the first plane of that sort shot down by a Hawk anywhere in the world.")[7]

Third Phase of U.S. Policy

American policy in the Middle East by now had evolved into a third phase, succeeding Mr. Truman's preference for Israel and General Eisenhower's even-handed approach, coupled with Secretary Dulles' effort to punish Nasser for bringing the Soviets into the Arab world. The third phase, which characterized the Kennedy and Johnson years, had several complex strands.

One was continuance of American friendship with Israel. Another was recognition of President Nasser as the dominant Arab leader, with whom Washington had to work, willy-nilly. Nothing, it was felt in Washington, would drive the Egyptian leader faster into external adventure than to support other Middle Eastern governments, while ignoring his. Stability in Egypt might be enhanced through an attack on the nation's overwhelming social problems, springing in part from Egypt's runaway population growth. A third policy strand was encouragement of King Hussein, to help keep the young monarch on his throne. Finally, American oil interests in Saudi Arabia and the Persian Gulf sheikdoms were to be protected.

Several episodes during this troubled period illustrated the intrusion of the Arab-Jewish conflict into domestic American affairs. On December 18, 1957, the American tanker *National Peace,* under contract to the U.S. Navy, was denied port facilities to pick up an oil cargo at Ras Tanura, Saudi Arabia. The Saudis

---

[6] This phrase, "attentive inactivity," was invented by Raymond A. Hare, United States Ambassador to Cairo during the post-Suez period.

[7] Associated Press, dateline Tel Aviv, May 21, 1969.

took the action because, under the name *S. S. Memory,* the tanker previously had traded with Israel. The navy canceled its contract with the *National Peace* and chose another vessel. Owners of the *National Peace* sued the navy for breach of contract and $160,000 damages.

To prevent a repetition, the navy began to insert the so-called "Haifa clause" into its oil tanker contracts. This gave the navy the right to cancel its charter if the tanker concerned were denied entry to an Arab port because of previous traffic with Israel. Navy authorities denied they were bowing to the Arab League boycott of Israel, though the clause in effect ruled out competition for contracts by American ships which had done business in Israeli ports. Congressional pressure caused the navy to agree on February 18, 1960, to eliminate the "Haifa clause" from future contracts.

Incidents like the above show how the Arab-Israel dispute has had repercussions on American institutions and American individuals, who in themselves have had little or no connection with the Palestine problem. This type of repercussion multiplied in the aftermath of the 1967 war, when Arab governments took various retaliatory measures against American interests, including temporary oil embargoes, the closing of certain cultural institutions, and the sequestration of property. Mention has been made of the fact that Egypt and six other Arab states broke diplomatic relations with Washington in 1967—a breach still unrepaired in 1970.

Yet President Nasser allowed the American University of Cairo to remain open, just as, in Lebanon, the American University of Beirut was permitted to continue. Despite the political rupture between some Arab governments and the United States, Arab leaders still appreciated the educational value to their own peoples of key American educational institutions in the Middle East.

On February 28, 1960, another abrasive issue arose, when the American Jewish Congress charged the State Department with having entered into "a gentleman's agreement" with Pakistan not to assign Jewish Americans to diplomatic or other posts in that country. This was in addition, the congress charged, to the Defense Department's "admitted" acceptance of a Saudi Arabian demand that no Jewish personnel be assigned to the U.S. air force base at Dhahran. The resolution went on to ask the United States Congress to investigate reports that the Agriculture Department and the Commodity Credit Corporation were refusing to ship U.S. government food stuffs to Egypt on ships which had traded with Israel. The goods involved were cargoes of surplus farm products sold under the Public Law 480 program.

State Department spokesman Lincoln White denied the allegation concerning Pakistan. Where Saudi Arabia was concerned, he pointed out the importance of the Dhahran base to American security and the fact that all personnel serving there had to obtain Saudi visas. "The Saudi Arabian Government," Mr. White added, "in exercise of its sovereign right to legislate and control internal matters has normally refused to issue entry visas to persons of Jewish faith irrespective of nationality." Far from condoning this discrimnatory action against American citizens, White continued, the State Department was making every effort to have such practices eliminated.

In all these instances it was Zionist agencies in the United States which complained that Washington, directly or indirectly, was favoring the Arabs. U.S. officials involved saw the matters differently. Taxpayers' money would be wasted, they stressed, if a ship which had done business with Israel were loaded with wheat, sent to Alexandria or another Arab port, only to be turned away.

An amendment to the government's 1960-61 foreign aid bill, passed by both houses of Congress, showed the opposite side of the coin. The amendment permitted the President to withhold foreign aid from any nation engaged in economic warfare against another country receiving American aid. Though the protagonists were not named, the amendment was aimed at denying U.S. economic assistance to Egypt, until Cairo opened the Suez Canal to Israeli ships.

Senator J. William Fulbright, chairman of the Senate Foreign Relations Committee, objected that the amendment amounted to "political coercion by the United States on behalf of one side to the long-smouldering Arab-Israeli dispute. It contemplates that the President is to use the Mutual Security Act as a club to force the United Arab Republic to open the Suez Canal to Israeli shipping." [8]

On April 13, 1960, the Seafarers International Union threw a picket line around the Egyptian ship *Cleopatra* in New York harbor. Stevedores of the International Longshoremen's Association refused to discharge her cargo. Paul Hall, head of the SIU, called the action a retaliation for the loss of American seamen's jobs as a result of the Arab boycott of Israel. Some American ship owners, according to Mr. Hall, were refusing to trade with the Jewish state, lest their vessels be blacklisted by the Arabs.

Arab trade union leaders, branding the *Cleopatra* incident a "Zionist-imperialist" plot, ordered a boycott of American shipping in all Arab ports, until the picket line was withdrawn from the Egyptian vessel. The Arab boycott was completely effective. American ships could not be unloaded in Arab ports, even though their cargoes included emergency wheat shipments destined for hungry Syrians, suffering from a third straight year of drought.

The SIU ended its picketing of the *Cleopatra* only after the State Department committed itself to seek an end to the blacklisting of American ships by the Arab League boycott office. In fact, there was little the State Department could do, except hope that the issue would not erupt again. Senator Fulbright described the *Cleopatra* incident and the congressional foreign aid amendment as "part of a pattern which I find disastrous to the functioning of our constitutional system. . . . In what is probably the most delicate international situation which exists in the world today, 180,000,000 Americans find their foreign policy being whipsawed by an irresponsible maritime union and by a minority pressure group." [9]

American labor leaders, including Mr. Hall of the SIU, denied that Zionist pressure had contributed to the *Cleopatra* case. American Zionist organizations added their denial. Indeed, some American Zionists and Israeli government officials feared the incident might boomerang against Israel, by arousing American resentment against the Jewish state. Such episodes, whatever elements may have been involved in individual cases, complicated the task of the U.S. government,

---

[8] Reuters, dateline Washington, May 7, 1960.
[9] *New York Times,* April 29, 1960.

striving at that time to restore an image of American impartiality in the Middle East.

American Stance in June 1967

By the spring of 1967 three American Presidents—Eisenhower, Kennedy, and Johnson—had fostered the concept of American neutrality between Arabs and Israelis. The more radical Arab governments did not accept this attitude as genuine and many American politicians continued to make flattering references to Israel and very few to the Arabs. Nonetheless, United States assistance to Middle Eastern countries was being divided more fairly between Arabs and Israelis than had been the case in the early 1950s.

This policy stemmed from the State Department's assessment that, not only must Arab nationalism be lived with, but it provided an effective barrier to Communist penetration. President Nasser, while accepting Soviet arms and mortgaging Egypt's cotton crops to pay for them, continued to crack down on Communists at home. No Arab government at the time of the June war was in serious danger of takeover by home-grown Communists.

Intent on avoiding a Middle Eastern arms race, the United States had resolved to sell only those weapons to Arabs and Israelis needed to restore a balance between them. The sale of Hawk missiles to Israel was a case in point, as was the sale of jet aircraft to King Hussein.

On May 23, 1967, two weeks before war broke out, President Johnson defined American policy as follows: "To the leaders of all the nations of the Near East, I wish to say what American Presidents have said before me—that the United States is firmly committed to the support of the political independence and territorial integrity of all nations of that area. The United States strongly opposes aggression by anyone in the area, in any form, overt or clandestine."

Mr. Johnson repeated this formula at a news conference in Washington June 13, when Israel's army had rewritten the Middle Eastern map. "That is our policy," the President declared, referring to his May 23 statement. "It will continue to be our policy. How it will be effectuated will be determined by the events of the days ahead."

This meant, as Israeli officials saw it, that the United States was committed to work for the withdrawal of Israeli forces from those parts of Syria, Jordan, and Egypt occupied in the lightning war. In fact, Washington's policy had been designed to cover more than Palestine. It was meant to shield Saudi Arabia, for example, against possible Egyptian aggression. But Israel's shattering military victory left the United States awkwardly exposed. According to Mr. Johnson's definition, Washington now was bound to hold that the Sinai Peninsula, including Sharm al-Sheik and the Gaza Strip, belonged to Egypt, just as the West Bank and the Old City of Jerusalem belonged to Jordan, and the Golan Heights to Syria. This interpretation was strengthened by President Johnson's statement that Arab-Israeli boundaries should not reflect the weight of conquest.

Should the United States press Israel to retreat, as President Eisenhower had done successfully in 1956? Washington took refuge in the unanimous November 22, 1967, Security Council resolution on the Middle East conflict.

This resolution called for Israeli withdrawal from territory occupied during the June war. But the U.N. document also recognized the right of all states to live in peace within secure and guaranteed borders. Taken together, these two points might permit a modification of Middle Eastern frontiers, if Arabs and Israelis could agree upon them. But no American official cared to define publicly where the new frontiers should be.

Before he left office President Johnson approved the sale of 50 F-4 Phantom jet fighters to Israel, at a price of $200 million. This deal was confirmed by President Nixon. Delivery of the aircraft began during 1969. The Phantom sale was designed to offset acquisition by the Egyptian air force of advanced Soviet fighters to replace those lost in 1967.

Israel, for its part, paid the United States $6,899,957 to compensate families of crewmen killed or injured, when Israeli planes and torpedo boats attacked the *U.S.S. Liberty* during the 1967 war. On June 8 the *Liberty*, a U.S. Navy intelligence-gathering ship crammed with electronic gear, was operating 15 miles off the Mediterranean coast of the Sinai Peninsula. The war was in full swing and presumably the *Liberty* was monitoring both Israeli and Egyptian communications, as well as any others in the area.

Suddenly Israeli craft assaulted the *Liberty* from sea and air, killing 34 American crewmen, wounding 164 others, and heavily damaging the vessel. Jewish officials later insisted the attack had been an accident. Some American sources expressed suspicion that the attack had been deliberate, to protect the security of Israeli communications. Whatever the case, Israel apologized, Washington accepted the apology, and the Israeli government paid compensation in two installments. Still to be worked out is recompense for damage to the ship itself.

In February 1968 Washington lifted its arms embargo on Jordan, imposed during the June war. In March 1968 King Hussein contracted to buy a squadron of F-104 jet interceptors, less advanced aircraft than the Phantoms. Following a visit to Washington by King Hussein in April 1969, President Nixon's Administration gave Jordan an option to buy a second squadron of F-104s.

Big Four Talks

On February 5, 1969, France suggested a four-power meeting on the Middle East, to which the United States agreed in principle. Washington had not abandoned its view that direct negotiations between Arabs and Israelis should precede a binding peace settlement. But months had passed with the two sides still far apart and the threshold of violence was mounting on the cease-fire lines.

Beginning in April representatives of the United States, the Soviet Union, Britain, and France began to meet periodically to map out the framework of a peace plan. Aware of Israeli disapproval, Joseph J. Sisco, U.S. Assistant Secretary of State for the Near East, described the talks as "a catalyst," for the purpose of "developing a substantive framework in which parties directly concerned can develop their dialogue."

The United States, in other words, did not intend to impose a settlement on the Middle East. The hope was that the Big Four—motivated by American and Soviet desire to avoid a major war—could establish the outline of a reasonable settlement. U.N. representatives in the Middle East then might persuade Arabs and Israelis to fill in the outline with specific details, while the Big Four exerted influence from the sidelines.

Noteworthy in this respect were remarks on the Arab refugee problem, delivered by Mr. Sisco in a speech April 24 before the American Israel Public Affairs Committee. "The refugees," declared the American official, "should be given a choice between repatriation and resettlement with compensation. There is a need for a fundamental solution which takes into account the human element and the concerns and requirements of both sides." [10] Israel's security needs were included in this assessment, Mr. Sisco made clear. Reportedly American officials would have liked the Zionist state to take back perhaps 100,000 refugees. The rest would be compensated, with United States help, and resettled in Arab host lands.

Israeli Prime Minister Golda Meir wrote to President Nixon to impress on him "some of the most undesirable consequences" of a possible Soviet-American agreement on the Middle East.[11] In particular she opposed what Israelis regard as the "tragic mistake" of 1956-57, when the United States and the Soviet Union forced Israel to withdraw from Sinai without a peace treaty. This, in the Israeli view, caused President Nasser to believe he could plan with impunity for a future war.

Big Four negotiations achieved few concrete results. This became clear when the Soviets rejected the draft of an initial United States peace plan, which American officials—after months of back and forth with the Soviets—had hoped might meet a favorable reception in Moscow. The American draft consisted of two parts—one dealing with Jordan-Israeli relations and the other with relations between Israel and the United Arab Republic. The latter plan was submitted for Soviet consideration on October 28, 1969, and the ideas concerning Jordan were given to the other members of the Big Four on December 18, 1969.

Essence of the American proposals was that Israel should withdraw unqualifiedly from all Arab territory seized during the June 1967 war, in return for an Arab pledge for a binding and permanent peace with the Jewish state. Israel should be guaranteed freedom of passage through international waterways. Palestinian refugees were to be given a choice between repatriation and compensation and Jordan and Israel should seek an agreement on control of Jerusalem and its holy places.

All this, the United States suggested, should be worked out in negotiations based on the Rhodes formula. Use of the term "Rhodes formula" was designed to blur the issue of whether Arabs and Israelis were in fact talking face to face. During the Rhodes talks in 1948-49, Ralph Bunche, the U.N. Mediator, had moved from Arabs to Israelis, who sat in separate rooms. Israel subsequently claimed that the Rhodes talks, which resulted in the armistice agreements of 1949, were direct Arab-Israeli negotiations. The Arabs disagreed.

In any event, Moscow rebuffed the American peace draft in a note delivered to Washington December 23, 1969. Describing the American proposals as "one-sided and pro-Israeli," the Soviet note also rejected the Rhodes formula as inexpedient, "in view of the sharp differences which have recently emerged in interpreta-

---

[10] Hedrick Smith, *New York Times,* April 24, 1969.
[11] Francis Ofner, *The Christian Science Monitor,* May 22, 1969.

tion" of the formula. American officials countered that the Soviet response of December 23 was a "retreat" from earlier positions thought to have been agreed upon.

Israel, too, rejected the American proposals, centering its objections on American suggestions for the future status of Jerusalem. Top Israeli officials declared that all of East Jerusalem now was open to Jewish settlement, that the Israeli government would aid Jews who wished to settle in the former Jordanian part of Jerusalem, and that Israel never would give up control of the unified city. Jerusalem, declared Deputy Premier Yigal Allon, had been unified legally "by Knesset action." [12] The Israelis repeated their insistence that final peace could be achieved only through direct Arab-Jewish negotiations, free of outside influence.

On January 31, 1970, Soviet Premier Aleksei N. Kosygin warned the Western powers to restrain Israel from further attacks on the Arab states. Otherwise, declared Mr. Kosygin, Moscow would be obliged to deliver new weapons to the Arabs. The Soviet warning was delivered in separate notes to the United States, Britain, and France. President Nixon's reply of February 4, 1970, repeated American willingness to work for binding peace between Arabs and Israelis, based on the earlier United States draft peace plan. Mr. Nixon also stressed American readiness to discuss the limitation of arms shipments to the Middle East.

As Soviet military involvement in Egypt heightened during the spring and summer of 1970, the United States updated its peace plan. Secretary of State William Rogers proposed a three-month cease-fire by Israel, Egypt, and Jordan, during which U.N. representative Gunnar V. Jarring again would seek implementation of the Security Council resolution of November 1967.

President Nasser, following a three-week stay in the Soviet Union, expressed qualified acceptance of the new American plan. So did Jordan. The Rogers plan prompted the Soviets to reshape their own proposals. The conclusion seemed to be that Moscow, while salving Nasser with more weapons deliveries, was exerting pressure on the Arabs to accept a political settlement.

Israel, however, foresaw danger in the three-month truce, charging that Soviets and Egyptians would use the time to strengthen their joint missile defenses west of the Suez Canal.

Finally, under intense diplomatic pressure, Golda Meir's government accepted the American cease-fire plan and Ambassador Jarring began his negotiations with the parties concerned. The cease-fire agreed to by Egypt, Jordan, and Israel went into effect August 7, 1970. However, hopes for peace in the Middle East were quickly dampened by the Egyptian-USSR violation of the "standstill" agreement and the hijacking of four commercial airplanes by a Palestinian commando group, unleashing the bloody Jordanian civil war.

In this whole situation, meanwhile, the United States labored under the handicap of having no diplomatic relations with seven Arab states—Egypt, Algeria, the Sudan, Syria, Iraq, Yemen, and South Yemen. On June 9, 1967, President Nasser had alleged over Cairo Radio that American and British planes operating from aircraft carriers in the Mediterranean had contributed to the UAR's defeat. This was

---

[12] *New York Times,* December 11, 1969.

untrue, as Mr. Nasser must have known. The Soviets, at any rate, did not believe their Arab ally in Cairo. President Johnson used the hot line to inform Mr. Kosygin that no American aircraft were involved. "We would have known if a fly had taken off from your carriers," a Soviet diplomat later confided to an American official.

Nonetheless, President Nasser, stuck with his own claim, severed diplomatic relations with the United States. Six other Arab governments followed suit—South Yemen more recently than the others—and at this writing ties have not been restored.

VI. OTHER POWERS AND ISRAEL

In 1960 American intelligence agents learned that France and Israel were constructing a 24,000-kilowatt nuclear reactor outside Dimona in the Negev. Neither government had informed the United States of this project, though Washington earlier had helped the Jewish state build a small 1,000-kilowat reactor near Tel Aviv. Despite Israeli assurances that the large reactor was intended for peaceful uses only, the United States found it difficult to penetrate the veil of secrecy cast about French-Israeli operations at Dimona.

This collaboration was the exposed tip of secret French-Israeli cooperation which, like an iceberg, ran deep. Public evidence of this emerged in 1956, when French pilots flew French jets for the Israeli air force in the Suez war of 1956. Following that war, France became for years Israel's chief military supplier.

At the outbreak of fighting in June 1967 Israel owned more than 200 combat aircraft, mostly acquired from France. These included 25 Vautour light jet bombers, 72 Mirage III-C fighter/bomber-interceptors, 20 Super Mystère fighter/interceptors, 40 Mystère IVA fighter-bombers, and 40 Ouragan fighter-bombers.[1] The Israeli army, by contrast, equipped with Centurion, Patton, Sherman, and Super Sherman tanks, still depended largely on the United States and Britain for its armor. An exception was the French-built AMX-13 light tank and the AML light armored car.

Between the 1956 and 1967 Arab-Jewish wars, the Israeli army maintained a permanent military mission attached to the French Ministry of Defense in Paris. French and Israeli intelligence officers exchanged visits and information. Israel was the only nation with a mission permanently attached to the French atomic energy commission. This cooperation began during the French Fourth Republic and continued unchecked after General de Gaulle came to power in 1958.

Background to this cooperation was the mutual antipathy of both powers to Arab policy in general and to President Nasser in particular. France, struggling to end its involvement in Algeria, was angered by Egyptian propaganda blasts against

---

[1] Geoffry Kemp, *Arms & Security: The Egypt-Israel Case* (London: The Institute for Strategic Studies, Adelphi Papers Number Fifty-Two, October 1968), p. 5.

65

French policy and even more by Mr. Nasser's hospitality to Algerian rebel leaders. Egypt also served as a transit point for arms smuggled to the Algerian National Liberation Front.

When Algeria gained its independence in 1962, French policy toward the Arabs —and vice versa—began to change. France sought to revive its traditional friendship with Arab peoples, using massive economic, technical, and financial aid to its former North African colonies to sweeten this policy. As a consequence, relations between France and Israel began to cool.

President de Gaulle blamed Israel for starting the 1967 June war and cut off French military shipments to the Jewish state. This embargo had two stages. Until January 3, 1969, Paris denied the sale of major weapons systems, including aircraft, but allowed the movement of spare parts to Israel. After January 3, in retaliation for Israeli's attack on Beirut Airport, Paris forbade the shipment of spare parts as well.

Particularly galling to Israel was an embargo on the delivery of 50 Mirage V supersonic jet interceptors, for which it had paid in full. At this writing the aircraft sit in hangars of the French firm Avions Marcel Dassault, which built them.

The resignation of President de Gaulle in the spring of 1969 promised a fresh start in French-Israeli relations. During his campaign to succeed de Gaulle, Georges Pompidou told members of the Israel-France Friendship League in Paris that "he would make changes in French Middle East policy." [2] Israel was invited to attend the 1969 Paris air show and Marcel Dassault expressed confidence that his company soon would be allowed to send the 50 Mirage aircraft to their Jewish owners.[3]

Mr. Dassault's confidence proved to be ill-founded. President Pompidou indeed made changes in French Middle Eastern policy, but in the direction of strengthening French-Arab ties. Vehicle for this maneuver was the desire of Libya's young military officers, who had deposed King Idris and established a Revolutionary Command Council (RCC) on September 1, 1969, to equip their armed forces with modern weapons.

Reports that France intended to sell Libya substantial numbers of aircraft caused the United States to make inquiries in Paris. French officials assured Washington that the total number of planes under consideration was ten to 15. The fact turned out to be otherwise. On January 21, 1970, French Defense Minister Michel Debré announced that France would sell 100 aircraft to the tiny Libyan air force. Delivery would be accomplished by 1974. The planes, according to Mr. Debré, would include 30 Mirage 3E jets, equipped for low-level blind flying and firing; 50 Mirage V jet interceptors (the same aircraft denied to Israel), and 20 training and reconnaissance aircraft.

The reasons advanced for the sale were two. First, Libya had not been an active participant in the 1967 war. Hence the self-imposed French arms embargo was not being violated. Second, if France were not to equip the Libyans, another power—by inference the Soviet Union—would do so. Since Libya, with only 1.8 million

---

[2] Israeli evening newspaper *Yediot Aharanot,* as quoted by Francis Ofner in *The Christian Science Monitor,* May 16, 1969.
[3] Reuters, dateline Paris, May 30, 1969.

people, had only a handful of jet-qualified pilots, the question arose whether the planes in some way would find their way into Egyptian hands. This was denied by the French government.

The French embargo caused Israel to make special efforts to buy compensatory arms from the United States. On July 7, 1968, Washington announced that the United States would sell more Hawk missiles to Israel, to supplement the first battalion. This was accompanied by the agreement to sell Israel 50 Phantom jet fighter-bombers, with delivery to start in 1970. President Nixon held open the possibility that additional sales would be authorized, if needed to maintain an arms balance.

Reports before the June war indicated that France and Israel were developing jointly a surface-to-surface missile, to fill a gap in Israel's arsenal. This missile, called the MD 620, with a range of 300 miles and a warhead of 1,000 pounds, presumably would carry a conventional warhead.[4]

American supporters of Israel demonstrated actively against French President Pompidou when he visited the United States in February-March 1970. They protested French policy which had shifted by then toward sympathy with Arab states, notably Libya. France also had refused to deliver Mirage jets to Israel even though they had been paid for.

President Nixon made an unscheduled trip to New York to see M. Pompidou to reinforce American official regard for France after particularly hostile demonstrations there, including an implied snub by the New York mayor.

Persistent press reports have alleged that Israel, using its Dimona reactor, has manufactured an atomic bomb. Prime Minister Golda Meir described these reports as "absolute fiction." "Israel has no nuclear bomb," Mrs. Meir affirmed. "Israel has no intention of using nuclear bombs." [5]

Some Western experts doubt that Mrs. Meir's denial tells the whole story. American sources claim the Dimona installations never have been fully opened to inspection by United States experts, though partial viewing has been allowed. "Western experts," wrote *The Christian Science Monitor*, "are growingly certain that Israel has nuclear-weapons capability and could manufacture them—if indeed it hasn't done so already. Top-secret Israeli installations at Dimona in the Negev Desert are thought to have made plutonium." [6]

The United Arab Republic has signed the nuclear nonproliferation treaty, which Israel has not. But President Nasser also has said that, if Israel introduced nuclear weapons into the Middle East, the United Arab Republic would acquire them also.

Israel and the Common Market

French-Israeli relations are closely allied to the Jewish state's efforts to obtain an association agreement with the European Economic Community (EEC, or Common Market). Israel sells goods worth about $200 million yearly to the EEC,

---

[4] Kemp, *op. cit.,* p. 10.
[5] Associated Press, dateline Jerusalem, May 9, 1969.
[6] *The Christian Science Monitor,* May 8, 1969.

but buys in return goods worth much more than that. Taken together, the six members of the Common Market buy nearly one-third of Israel's total exports.

These exports must climb over the common external tariff barrier erected by the EEC against outside powers. In 1964 the EEC concluded a special agreement with Israel, granting tariff concessions on a wide variety of exports. "Nonetheless," remarked an Israeli economist, "EEC tariffs on our exports average 15 to 25 percent, against zero tariffs inside the Common Market itself."

In 1966 Israel applied for associate membership of the EEC, similar to that achieved by Greece and Turkey. Five members of the Common Market support the Israeli application, though they differ on how far trade preferences should go. Holland and West Germany want a global agreement on Israeli commerce, while Italy would limit preferences to 40 percent of industrial trade. But France has held out against any preferences at all, with the result that Israel's application has bogged down. Israeli officials hope that the French attitude may soften under the post-de Gaulle regime.

Meanwhile, early in 1970 widened tariff concessions were granted to Israel, liberalizing the 1964 agreement. The new preferential tariff arrangements are scheduled to run for five years, during which period Israel will continue to press its application for association with the EEC.

West Germany

"Relations between Israel and West Germany are positive," commented a senior Israeli diplomat. "Our economic relations are close and Germany's attitude in 1967 meant a lot to us. But," he hesitated, "a mortgage remains on those relationships which cannot be wholly paid off."

He referred to the obvious fact that Jews cannot forget the slaughter of six million of their brethren by Germans of the Third Reich. Conscious of its debt to the Jews, the West German government in manifold ways has tried to make amends. On September 10, 1952, Chancellor Konrad Adenauer and Israeli Foreign Minister Moshe Sharett signed an agreement in Luxembourg. This provided for a total payment by the Federal Republic to the state of Israel of $862 million, to be divided into 14 yearly installments.

This money was used to buy goods in West Germany and send them to Israel. Five categories of products were included—iron, steel, and nonferrous metals; processed steel goods; products of the chemical and other industries; agricultural products; and services, including the price of transport to Israel, insurance of the goods, and costs incurred by the Israeli mission in Cologne, which supervised the transactions.

This agreement expired March 31, 1966. Bonn then promised to give Israel economic aid for an indefinite period, reportedly at an average of more than $30 million yearly. In 1968 and 1969 West Germany loaned Israel a total of $70 million, designed to help the Jewish state expand its road system, build new housing, improve telephone and telegraphic communications, and modernize Lod airport. Some money went to Israel's industrial development bank. These loans were not tied to purchases of German goods.

West Germany is Israel's third most important trading partner, after the United States and Britain. In 1969 Israel exported goods worth $65 million to the Federal Republic, an increase of 14 percent over the year before. In 1969 the Jewish state bought $132 million worth of German goods, against $102 million in 1968.

The largest category of West German aid is restitution to individual Israelis for suffering and losses experienced under Hitler. These payments—wholly apart from the Adenauer-Sharett agreement—began in 1954 and totaled $1,965 million by the end of 1967. These cash payments were in two forms, lump-sum compensations and annual pensions to victims of the Third Reich. Restitution of this kind continues and will go on so long as individual recipients are alive.[7]

In March 1965 the West German government decided to open diplomatic relations with Israel. Chancellor Ludwig Erhard sent a special emissary, parliamentary deputy Kurt Birrenbach, to Israel to discuss the matter with Jewish leaders. On March 14, 1965, the Israeli government accepted in principle the German offer of recognition.

The decision had been hard for both sides. "The catastrophe which befell the Jewish people during the Nazi regime," Prime Minister Levi Eshkol told the Knesset during debate on the question, "has given a very special meaning to every action or omission on the part of the Germans which is likely to damage the status of the Israeli state or the feelings of the Jewish people. . . . We have never given up hope that Germany would be able to free herself from the terrible heritage of the past in the eyes of the world and would build a new foundation for her relationship with Israel and to the Jewish people." [8]

For Israelis the problem centered on whether or not to extend a hand of friendship to the people who had caused the Jews so much suffering. For West Germans the question was different. To that point Bonn held primacy over East Berlin in the Arab world. Generous technical and economic aid programs had given the Federal Republic a strong foothold in Arab capitals. Representation of Walter Ulbricht's Communist East German regime, by contrast, was minimal. But Bonn officials knew that Arab governments would react in anger to West German recognition of Israel and that the German Democratic Republic (GDR) might reap the benefit. Nonetheless, there was no question that morally West Germany had to recognize Israel.

Diplomatic relations were established May 12, 1965; Bonn sent Rolf Pauls, a distinguished diplomat and a former officer of the Wehrmacht, as its first ambassador to the Jewish state. Greeted with jeers and hostility by some embittered Israelis when he arrived, Mr. Pauls left nearly four years later with the esteem and respect of the Israeli people. Today Pauls is West German Ambassador to the United States.

Israel's choice to send to Bonn was Asher Ben-Natan, a tough, athletic, former intelligence agent, who, after World War II, had headed the Austrian branch of the Jewish Agency for Palestine's Operation Flight. There he had helped to gather

---

[7] Oded Remba, "The Dilemmas of Israel's Economy," *Midstream*, February 1969, pp. 55–56.
[8] As quoted by Theo M. Loch, *Meet Germany* (Hamburg: Atlantik-Brucke, January 1966), p. 44.

Jewish survivors of Nazi concentration camps for transportation to Palestine. Later he did much of the spadework that led to the tracking down and capture of Adolph Eichmann.

Chiefs of government of each of the 13 Arab League member states received a letter from Chancellor Erhard, outlining Bonn's point of view. In no way, the letters stressed, was Bonn's recognition of Israel designed to injure West Germany's traditionally friendly relations with the Arabs. Rather it was another step toward the closing of a deeply painful chapter of German-Jewish history.

Nonetheless, ten members of the Arab League severed diplomatic relations with the Federal Republic. They were Algeria, Egypt, Iraq, Jordan, Kuwait, Lebanon, Saudi Arabia, the Sudan, Syria, and Yemen. Only Tunisia, Morocco, and Libya kept their ambassadors in Bonn. King Hussein of Jordan subsequently reopened his embassy in West Germany, as did Yemen. Eight Arab governments maintain their break.

Disclosure of a secret German-Israeli arms deal, whereby Bonn had contracted to sell the Jewish state an estimated $80 million worth of weapons, added to Arab anger. Key figures in arranging this deal were Franz Josef Strauss, then West German Defense Minister, and Mr. Ben-Natan, at that time representing the Israeli Ministry of Defense in Paris. When the agreement was exposed, the resulting agitation caused Bonn to cancel the deal. Israel was promised economic compensation, estimated at about $15 million, for the undelivered portion of arms.

In part the sale of weapons to Israel had been intended to offset Israeli unease over the presence of German scientists working in Egypt. These scientists, numbering more than 200 citizens of the Federal Republic and Austria, were helping the UAR develop at least two types of ground-to-ground rockets, whose launching sites were being spotted throughout the Sinai Peninsula. Other West German technicians reportedly were working with Swiss firms and the Spanish branch of Messerschmitt to develop air frames and jet engines for Egyptian aircraft.

These varied activities caused the Israeli government to demand in March 1963 that West Germany forbid its nationals to work on weapons development in the United Arab Republic. Such a bar on private citizens was impossible, Bonn replied, under the Federal Republic Constitution. However, West German leaders in and out of government—including Mr. Strauss—sought to find jobs at home for West German technicians in Egypt, a task made difficult by the high salaries paid by Cairo.

The full scale of West German military assistance to Israel never has been disclosed. In May 1963 Shimon Peres, Israel's deputy defense minister, declared that Bonn's contributions to Israel's vital defense needs were no less important than those of France. On the face of it this was an extraordinary statement, since France at that time was in the full flush of furnishing sophisticated weapons systems to the Jewish state.

Following Mr. Peres' statement, West German parliamentary sources in Bonn disclosed that Israeli troops were receiving training in Germany. Reportedly some Israeli soldiers had entered West Germany in French uniform, suggesting a three-cornered French-German-Israeli collaboration. The West German army also helped Israel's defense industry by ordering large numbers of the Israeli-made Uzzi submachine gun.

The United States came in for a surprise on this score, when officials discovered that some American military equipment, including helicopters assigned to West Germany under NATO, had been shipped clandestinely to Israel. A stern American protest elicited a promise from Bonn that this would not happen again.

West Germany continues to pay a price for its friendship with Israel. In the spring and summer of 1969 five Arab governments—Egypt, Syria, Iraq, the Sudan, and South Yemen—exchanged ambassadors with Ulbricht's GDR. These states, plus Cambodia, were the first non-Communist powers to recognize the East German regime. The Syrian and East German foreign ministers, concluding their diplomatic compact in Damascus in June 1969, termed it an "annihilating blow against the imperialist alliance between Israel and West Germany." Bonn replied that the offending Arab states had destroyed the possibility of restoring normal relations between themselves and the Federal Republic. Nonetheless, Bonn would continue to work for good relations with those Arab countries which kept aloof from the GDR.

West Germany is punished by the Arabs for trying to make amends to the Jews, while the GDR is rewarded for having done nothing for Israel. Mr. Ulbricht's government has refused to pay compensation to Israel or to individual Jews, claiming that the Federal Republic, not Communist East Germany, was the successor to Hitler's Third Reich. The GDR, scrambling for Arab favor, accused Israel of waging aggressive war against the Arabs in 1967.

Great Britain

Britain's involvement in Palestine up through the mandate period already has been substantially discussed. Paramount as an influence in the early days of Zionism and during the mandate, Britain largely withdrew from the Palestine arena in 1948. Subsequently Britain joined with France and the United States in signing the 1950 Tripartite Declaration. In 1956 Britain reemerged on the Middle Eastern scene, as a participant in the brief Suez war.

Prime minister and chief executor of Britain's Suez role in 1956 was Sir Anthony Eden, later Lord Avon. As Winston Churchill's understudy for many years, Eden had built a reputation for responsible statesmanship. He had, for example, deplored the Western appeasement of Hitler in the Munich Agreement of 1938 and had warned of dangerous consequences to come. Eden's policy as prime minister during the Suez episode was based on his conviction that the appetite of dictators must be curbed. A number of times during the troubled fall of 1956 Eden compared Nasser and his ambitions with those of Hitler and Mussolini. To Eden it seemed clear that Nasser's nationalization of the Suez Canal must be revoked.

Seizure of the Suez Canal by the Egyptian leader, Eden wrote, was "the opening gambit in a planned campaign designed by Nasser to expel all Western influence and interests from Arab countries. He believes that if he can get away with this. . . his prestige in Arabia will be so great that he will be able to mount revolutions

of young officers in Saudi Arabia, Jordan, Syria, and Iraq. . . . These new Governments will in effect be Egyptian satellites if not Russian ones. They will have to
place their united oil resources under the control of a united Arabia led by Egypt
and under Russian influence. When that moment comes Nasser can deny oil to
Western Europe and we here shall all be at his mercy." [9]

From this premise Eden led Great Britain into an alliance with France and
Israel, resulting in the three-pronged attack on Egypt in 1956. Israel's prime
motive, as we have seen, was to rid the Sinai Peninsula of Arab commando bases
and of Egyptian army positions. France and Britain hoped to restore the Suez
Canal to Western control and, in the process, possibly to topple President Nasser
from power. London's intervention deeply divided public opinion in Britain, much
as the Vietnam war later was to do in the United States.

Throughout this period Eden felt himself undercut by the United States, and in
particular by Secretary of State John Foster Dulles. The British government
believed Dulles' decision to cancel the Aswan Dam deal was abruptly reached,
without prior consultation with Britain. Following Mr. Nasser's nationalization of
the Suez Canal, Eden felt that the United States failed to back up Britain in put-
ting sufficient pressure on Egypt to force Nasser to "disgorge" the canal. Eden
cited as one example the United States decision to freeze only the dollar balances
of the Egyptian government and the National Bank of Egypt, but not new receipts
in these accounts, nor dollar accounts held by private Egyptians.

Eden further was convinced that President Eisenhower and Mr. Dulles both signaled clearly to President Nasser American reluctance—indeed refusal—to contemplate the use of force against Egypt, if all other methods to regain the waterway
were to fail. Meanwhile, Australian Prime Minister Robert Menzies, who had led a
special mission to Cairo at Sir Anthony's request, could not negotiate a settlement
with President Nasser. Still convinced of the Egyptian leader's anti-Western intentions, and deeply alarmed by the implications to Europe of loss of Arab oil, Eden
and the French government, together with Israel, secretly compacted to make war.
The outbreak of hostilities, as we have seen, led to intense American pressure on
its two European allies, as well as on Israel, to withdraw from Egyptian soil. The
Suez adventure, in addition to straining British-American relations, effectively
broke Sir Anthony's career.

In the years that followed, Britain has been active as an arms supplier to the
Middle East, notably to Jordan and Israel, but not on the scale of the United
States, the Soviet Union, and France. It was Britain which introduced the now-
famous U.N. resolution of November 22, 1967, centerpiece of current diplomatic
efforts. On the whole, however, recent British governments have failed to play a
leading role in the Arab-Israel dispute.

The Soviet Union

On June 10, 1967, while the Israeli army was mopping up Syrian resistance on
the Golan Heights, the Soviet Union broke diplomatic relations with the Jewish
state. A Soviet note on the occasion accused Israel of "continued aggression"

---

[9] Sir Anthony Eden, *Full Circle* (London: Cassell & Company Ltd., 1960), p. 465.

toward the Arabs and threatened "sanctions together with all consequences arising from them" against the State of Israel. This action followed a meeting in Moscow, at which seven Communist nations signed a statement promising aid and support to the Arabs, if Israel did not withdraw from conquered territory. Poland, Hungary, Czechoslovakia, Bulgaria, and Yugoslavia followed the Soviet lead and severed relations with Israel. Only Romania refused to sign the statement and to break relations with Israel.

Earlier, when the war broke out on June 5, the Soviets had opposed a U.N. Security Council resolution calling for a cease-fire and a withdrawal of both Arab and Israeli forces. Only on June 7, when the magnitude of Egyptian defeat became apparent, did Moscow accept a United States call for an unconditional cease-fire. The cease-fire resolution finally passed by the Security Council was sponsored by the Soviet Union. The inference was that Moscow wanted no cease-fire while its Arab clients had a chance of winning, but wanted the fighting to stop before the Arabs collapsed completely.

The postwar period was marked by a two-pronged Soviet policy. One was to rearm the Egyptians and to increase the number of Soviet advisers in the UAR. This was accompanied by a bolstering of the Soviet Mediterranean fleet. The second phase of Moscow's policy featured a consistent propaganda hammering of Israel within the United Nations.

All this, however, was to be kept within the bounds of preventing a new outbreak of war, which might jar the United States into action. Fear of American-Soviet confrontation in the Middle East induced the Soviets to endorse Big Four talks to find a political solution. In fact, Moscow initially was more eager than Washington to explore a Big Four avenue.

Concern about the danger of war led the Soviets to criticize fedayeen movements with growing sharpness. On June 6, 1969, the Soviet Communist party newspaper *Pravda* warned Arab commandos not to use military means to recapture territory held by Israel. Only through political methods, wrote *Pravda,* could lost lands be restored to the Arabs. Guerrilla propaganda, calling for total victory over the Zionist state, *Pravda* declared, helped Israel "to frustrate a political settlement." [10] The *Pravda* article, written by Middle East specialist V. Rumyantsev, was one of many indications of Soviet disquiet over the growing militancy and influence of the commando movement.

The Soviet Union had not always been hostile to Israel. In 1947 Moscow had supported the U.N. partition plan and the next year swiftly followed the United States in granting recognition to the Jewish state. At that time Soviet diplomats even attacked the Arabs for interfering with the United Nations partition scheme. During the period of Israel's creation, the Soviet Union was heavily arming Zionist forces, through the underground, and also through Czechoslovakia. Golda Meir became Israel's first ambassador to Moscow.

A turning point came about 1955, when Soviet leaders decided to use the Arab-Israeli conflict to lever themselves into the Middle East. This coincided with a wave of anti-Semitism in Russia during Stalin's closing years of life and immedi-

---

[10] Bernard Gwertzman, *New York Times,* June 6, 1969.

ately thereafter. A bomb thrown at the Soviet Embassy in Tel Aviv caused Moscow to break diplomatic relations with Israel in October 1953—the first of three such ruptures.

Contributing to Soviet policy at this time was the rise of President Nasser and the latter's growing opposition to Western activities in the Middle East, centered on the Baghdad Pact. Moscow's opportunity came when Nasser turned to the Soviets for fresh supplies of weapons, having failed to obtain them from the United States. Today the United Arab Republic, Syria, Iraq, Algeria, Yemen, and the People's Republic of Southern Yemen are wholly or partly dependent on Moscow for military equipment.

South Yemen, with its key port of Aden, is receiving a strong dose of Soviet attention. Western analysts foresee a Soviet effort to develop a base of operations in South Yemen, linking Soviet fleets in the Indian Ocean and the Mediterranean Sea. For easy communication between the two fleets Moscow wants the Suez Canal reopened.

The Soviets resumed diplomatic relations with Israel after their 1953 break, closed their Tel Aviv embassy again because of the 1956 Sinai war, then reestablished contact once more. Soviet diplomats apparently valued the opportunity to talk directly with Jewish officials, if only to sound out Israeli policy. The third diplomatic break, which still exists, came in June 1967.

Roughly two and one-half million Jews, more than in Israel itself, live in the Soviet Union. This is the world's second largest concentration of Jews, after the United States. A number of Soviet scientists prominent in Russian space programs and allied technology are Jewish. This, plus membership of many Jewish intellectuals in the Communist party, does not prevent periodic resurgence of the anti-Semitism which lurks beneath the Russian surface. Refusal to allow its Jewish citizens to emigrate, however, may be due more to Moscow's pro-Arab policy than to anti-Semitism.

A recent example of denigration of the Jews was the publication in Kiev of *Judaism and Zionism,* by Trofim Kichko, known for an earlier blatantly anti-Semitic book called *Judaism Without Embellishment.* The thrust of Kichko's new book was to discredit all religion, using Judaism as an example. The book also accused Zionists and the State of Israel of conspiring with imperialist enemies of the Soviet Union. The author singled out non-Zionist Soviet Jews for praise and argued that Jews as an ethnic group were not being attacked, but only Judaism as a religion and Zionists as a political body.

On balance, some Western analysts describe the current phase of anti-Semitism in the Soviet Union as depressing, but not virulent. They point to the fact that, according to *Sovietish Heimland,* a Yiddish-language monthly, "hundreds of books by Jewish writers have been published in the Soviet Union in the past few years with a circulation of over 30 million." [11] In February 1969 *Sovietish Heimland* also brought out an improved version of *An Aid to Those Studying Yiddish.* This was hailed by the American Jewish Congress as a "real breakthrough,"

---

[11] Paul Wohl, *The Christian Science Monitor,* May 15, 1969.

because it would give many young Soviet Jews an opportunity to obtain a reading grasp of Yiddish.

What Israelis would like, and what the Kremlin will not allow, is permission for Soviet Jews to emigrate freely to Israel. In June 1969 Kaia Helmut, a Soviet official in charge of issuing passports for emigration to Israel, announced that Moscow was continuing to allow Soviet Jews to leave "so as to reunite separated families." The number of Jews permitted to go to Israel under this pledge is believed to be small.

Poland also has been reluctant to let its Jewish citizens leave for Israel. For years Polish Jews found it almost impossible to emigrate. Then, following the Arab-Israel war in 1967, Polish Communist party chief Wladyslaw Gomulka warned Polish Jews against becoming a "fifth column." Emigration procedures were relaxed and from July 1, 1967 through May 1969, 5,264 Polish Jews left the country.[12] Their exit visas specified Israel as their destination, though some—once outside Poland—traveled to West Germany and to other Western lands.

This development coincided with a widespread anti-Semitic campaign within Poland. Many Jewish intellectuals, in government and out, lost their positions. Reportedly so many Jewish scientists were fired that the Polish atomic commission was virtually paralyzed.[13]

On June 10, 1969, the Polish government announced that liberal emigration policies for Jews would end on September 1. Applications by Polish Jews to leave the country after that date, according to the government press agency PAP, would be considered under stricter rules. Officially this remains Polish government policy. Nonetheless, a quiet exodus of Polish Jews continues, many of them traveling first to Scandinavia and then on to Israel and other points. Nearly 2,000 Polish Jews have chosen to remain in Denmark. Another large group went to Sweden, and others to Canada, Australia, and other lands. Unofficial but authoritive sources claim as many as 11,000 Jews may have left Poland since mid-1967. The same sources say about half these people have gone to Israel.

In 1968 Mr. Gomulka said there were an estimated 25,000-30,000 Jews in Poland. Israeli government sources put the total in mid-1969 at 22,000. Informed sources involved in channeling the emigrants from Poland to new homelands claim there now are fewer than 20,000 Jews left in Poland.

The Soviet Union, within the Big Four talks, is believed to be aiming at a staged withdrawal of Israeli troops from territories siezed in 1967. In return, Israel's Arab neighbors would deposit with the United Nations assurances concerning other aspects of the November 22 resolution, including the right of all states to live within secure and recognized boundaries and freedom to use international waterways in the Middle East.

Details of Soviet policy may change as negotiations proceed. But the Kremlin appears ready to entertain a compromise agreement, with the ultimate goals of preventing a new war, safeguarding Soviet interests in the Arab world, and opening the Suez Canal to permit a linkup between Russian fleets in Middle Eastern and South Asian waters.

---

[12] Associated Press, dateline Warsaw, quoting Polish press agency PAP, June 10, 1969.
[13] Ritchie McEwan, *The Times* (London), February 7, 1969.

Israel's relations with African and other developing nations deserve a special word. During the first decade of Israel's technical assistance program—from 1958 through 1968—more than 10,500 trainees from over 80 countries in Africa, Asia, and Latin America took part in seminars and courses of instruction in Israel. This remarkable achievement for so small a country was founded on a hardheaded political assessment.

Israeli leaders had been dismayed by President Nasser's success in obtaining an anti-Israel statement at the Bandung conference in Indonesia in 1955. At subsequent international gatherings the Egyptians achieved similar success. Israelis attributed this to almost total ignorance of the Jewish state among Africans and Asians. Foreseeing the coming independence of African countries, and foreseeing also that Nasser would attempt to freeze Israel out of the continent, the Israeli government resolved to move first.

In 1956 Israel opened a consulate at Accra, capital of the Gold Coast, and raised this to an embassy when Ghana became independent. As other African states gained their sovereignty Israel opened missions in their capitals, with the result that Israel today enjoys diplomatic relations with all African countries south of the Sahara, except Mauretania, Guinea, and Somalia.

Land reclamation and irrigation, increase of crop productivity, technical training in a variety of small industries—these are special skills which Israelis, drawing on their own experience, can impart to others. The resulting programs take many forms, with Jewish "Point Four" missions traveling to underdeveloped countries and the latter sending their students to Israel for training. Jewish experts helped Congo-Brazzaville and Congo-Kinshaha to develop poultry breeding, the Chad to establish a printing press, Liberia to open an eye clinic, Uganda to grow citrus fruits, and so on.

Joint companies to promote shipping and foreign trade, construction, and water supply and irrigation have been established by Israel with Asian and African governments. Generally the Israeli partner transfers its share of ownership to the developing country, when the joint enterprise is on its feet.

Political fruits of this policy became apparent at the African chiefs of state conference at Addis Ababa in 1963. Attending the conference was President Nasser of the UAR. Also at Addis Ababa were black African leaders, many of whom had visited Israel personally. As it happened, President Ahmadou Ahidjo of Cameroon flew directly to the conference from Israel, where he had been making a state visit.

Several African leaders warned President Nasser not to press for an anti-Israel resolution at Addis Ababa. "We are friendly with Israel," the Negro presidents told him in effect. "You are not. That is your business, but do not inject a personal note into Addis. If you do, you will split Africa in two. You will carrry white (Arab) Africa and we will carry black Africa. We would never forgive you for splitting Africa this way." [14]

---

[14] Harry B. Ellis, page 113 of chapter entitled "The Arab-Israeli Conflict Today" in *The United States and the Middle East,* edited by Georgiana G. Stevens and published by The American Assembly, 1964.

The fact that many of these Negro leaders were Moslem, as was Mr. Nasser and other Arab participants at Addis, did not incline the black presidents to the Arab view. They valued the technical assistance their countries had derived from Israel, a state which—in black African eyes—bore no imperialist taint, as did Britain, France, and other major powers which had ruled Africa in pre-independence days.

VII. UNITED NATIONS AND ISRAEL

More than any other country Israel is a child of the United Nations, for it was a majority vote of the world body which created a Jewish state in Palestine. Since then the Arab-Israeli conflict has preoccupied the attention of the United Nations more than any other international issue.

The United Nations Special Committee on Palestine, as we have seen, had recommended partition of Palestine and the historic vote supporting partition already had been taken, when Britain laid down its League of Nations mandate and transferred the problem to the United Nations. When fighting broke out, the United Nations Security Council appointed a mediator—first Count Bernadotte, then Ralph Bunche of the United States. To Mr. Bunche fell the task of negotiating armistice agreements on the island of Rhodes between Israel and its Arab neighbors.

Once these agreements had been signed, the next requirement was to keep the armistice lines intact. To this end a United Nations Truce Supervision Organization (UNTSO) was formed to act as a buffer along Arab-Israeli frontiers. This organization, commanded by a general officer appointed by the United Nations, was divided into separate teams of military observers, called Mixed Armistice Commissions (MAC). Each segment of border—Lebanon-Israel, Syria-Israel, and so on—had its own MAC, consisting of Arab and Israeli officers under a neutral chairman. Task of the Mixed Armistice Commissions was to mediate frontier disputes, stop fighting when it occurred, and report their findings to the United Nations in New York.

Creation of the United Nations Emergency Force (UNEF) after the Suez war in 1956 was an extension of this type of work. UNEF's task was twofold—to patrol the frontier between Israel and Egypt and to prevent the rearming of Egyptian shore batteries at the entrance of the Gulf of Aqaba. Israel's conquest of Sinai in 1967 moved the truce line west to the Suez Canal. United Nations peacekeeping forces were stationed at the Canal, but seemed powerless to prevent artillery duels and air battles from breaking out between Egyptian and Israeli forces.

Gunnar V. Jarring, Swedish Ambassador to Moscow, was appointed United Nations representative in the Middle East, charged with carrying out the terms of the November 22, 1967, Security Council resolution. U.N. Secretary-General U Thant defined Mr. Jarring's mission was establishing and maintaining "contacts with the states concerned in order to promote agreement and assist efforts to achieve a peaceful and accepted settlement."

Months of fruitless shuttling back and forth between Middle Eastern capitals by Mr. Jarring brought the two sides visibly no closer to agreement. At this point the Big Four resolved to seek a settlement on their own. Mr. Jarring remains aloof from this effort, on the conviction of all concerned that his effectiveness will be increased by noninvolvement with the major powers. Presumably the Swedish envoy will step back into the picture, if and when the Big Four develop recommendations which Mr. Jarring might transmit to the disputants. This is the aim of the latest American peace proposal.

Needs of Refugee Youth

These peacekeeping activities by the United Nations were supplemented by the creation in December 1948 of the United Nations Relief for Palestine Refugees, which in 1950 became UNRWA, or the United Nations Relief and Works Agency for Palestine Refugees in the Near East.

The twin functions of United Nations Relief Work Agency are indicated by two words in its name—relief and works. On the one hand, year by year and to an increasing number of people, administrators of UNRWA struggle to provide basic clothing, shelter, and food for hundreds of thousands of refugees. Before the 1967 war, this effort consumed each year more than $25 million of UNRWA's total budget of about $38 million, all raised by voluntary subscriptions from U.N. member countries. The uprooting of more people in 1967, according to UNRWA Commissioner-General Laurence Michelmore, requires the agency's annual budget to be raised to $43 million, if UNRWA is simply to maintain its earlier level of activities.

Little is left over for the "works" aspect of UNRWA's job—the training of young refugees to acquire skills which might carry them out of camps and into the mainstream of Arab life. Dr. John H. Davis, then commissioner-general of UNRWA, drew attention to the plight of young refugees in his 1962 report to the General Assembly. Half the refugees on UNRWA relief rolls, Dr. Davis wrote, were boys and girls under 17 years of age. Maturing at the rate of 30,000 per year, these young people were growing up almost completely devoid of work skills. Their parents, formerly farmers, small businessmen, or unskilled workers in Palestine, had been unable to find productive work in Arab host lands after 1948.

Children had no opportunity to learn trades from their parents and, what was more, had not gained the basic self-discipline that would make them employable, even if jobs could be found. "Therefore it would seem," Dr. Davis wrote, "that a high percentage of the young refugees who have grown to adulthood during the past fourteen years are destined to be handicapped for life, even when they have placed before them what to persons with normal backgrounds would be challenging opportunities."

Dr. Davis' further conclusion was that the economic situation of Arab host lands in most cases would not permit massive resettlement of refugees. A majority of these people, therefore, eventually would have to cross an international frontier to find work. This presupposed the possession of work skills.

To meet this need at least partially UNRWA under Dr. Davis and later commissioners-general concentrated on general and vocational education of refugee boys and girls. At latest count 180,000 refugee children were attending schools administered by UNRWA and UNESCO (United Nations Educational, Scientific and Cultural Organization), while 3,300 more were studying at UNRWA's centers for vocational and teacher training. (More than 50,000 other refugee youngsters were going to school in their Arab host lands.)[1]

The total number of young refugees studying at UNRWA vocational training schools is about one-tenth the number of young Palestinians who mature each year. This indicates the inadequacy of present efforts. But UNRWA's 100-member international staff and 11,900 Arab staff are convinced that providing work skills is the most meaningful way to begin to move the Palestine refugee problem off dead center, at least until Arabs and Israelis themselves achieve a solution. Without more money, however, UNRWA is sharply limited in this field.

The United Nations as a whole is in precarious financial situation, partly because of the refusal of the Soviet Union and France to pay their allotted shares of the world body's peacekeeping expenses. Under these circumstances the United Nations seems unlikely to extract significantly more money from its members to finance vocational training schools for UNRWA. Over the years the United States —which contributed $22 million toward UNRWA's 1969 budget—has furnished about 70 percent of the agency's total governmental contributions.

Hammarskjold and Johnson Reports

At various times the U.N. General Assembly has sought special guidance on the refugee problem from sources outside UNRWA. In 1959 Secretary-General Dag Hammarskjold was asked by the General Assembly to recommend how the refugees could be reintegrated "into the economic life of the Near East, either by repatriation or resettlement."

Hammarskjold cited the low per capita income of the four Arab host countries, ranging at that time from $128 yearly in Egypt to $364 in Lebanon. Given the rapid increase of Arab populations, the then secretary-general foresaw the need to pump $1.5 billion into these lands over the next five years, if living standards of their indigenous populations were to be raised at all.

To create additional jobs for the Palestine refugee work force would require a further $1.5 billion of outside help. The Hammarskjold report now is ten years old. Since then indigenous Arab populations, especially that of Egypt, have grown and so has the total of refugees. These factors alone would add to the international settlement bill forecast by the late Mr. Hammarskjold.

In 1948 the United Nations had created, along with UNTSO and UNRWA, a three-nation Conciliation Commission for Palestine (PCC), consisting of the

---

[1] United Nations Office of Public Information, Press Release PAL/1118, September 11, 1968.

81

United States, France, and Turkey. This body was charged with continuing the work of the U.N. mediator and to assume whatever other tasks the General Assembly might thrust upon it. In 1961 the PCC engaged Joseph E. Johnson, president of the Carnegie Endowment for International Peace, to make a fresh study of the refugee problem.

Dr. Johnson established first, as others before him had done, that Israel and the Arab governments could not agree on the number of refugees who should be allowed to return to Palestine, in lieu of compensation. He was forced, therefore, to make his recommendations somewhat in a vacuum, using as guidelines the human needs of the refugee population and the economic and security concerns of the countries directly involved. Since the United Nations itself had brought Israel into being, Dr. Johnson reasoned, the General Assembly—through its basic resolution 194/III of 1948 concerning refugees—had not intended a solution that would destroy or threaten the Jewish state. But certainly the General Assembly had had in mind the wishes of the Palestinians who had lost their homes.

Dr. Johnson suggested that refugee heads of families, insulated by the United Nations from outside pressure, should be allowed to opt freely for repatriation or compensation. The choices were to be made specific. Each head of family would be told what opportunities for resettlement existed in Israel and how much he would receive as compensation if he chose to take his family elsewhere. Compensation was to be based on 1947-48 property values in Palestine, plus accrued interest. United Nations member states, substantially the United States but also Israel, would furnish the compensation. Israel would be allowed to run a security check on each refugee choosing to return.

The Johnson proposal was rejected by both sides, though neither Arabs nor Israelis attacked the plan directly. Golda Meir, then Israeli foreign minister, recalled a Knesset resolution of November 1961, which stated there could be no returning of the Palestine refugees to Israel and that the only hope of solution lay in their integration in Arab lands. Arab governments, for their part, insisted again that Israel first must accept in principle the pertinent U.N. resolution of 1948.

Twenty years and two wars later the United Nations, as part of its five-point resolution of November 1967, included a "just settlement of the refugee problem" as an essential ingredient of Arab-Israeli peace. Today the problem is magnified, not only because there are more refugees, but by the enlistment of thousands of young Palestinians in al-Fatah and other resistance groups. These organized guerrillas project a threat to the internal stability of Arab governments, as well as to Middle Eastern peace.

The Conciliation Commission for Palestine (PCC) has accomplished two tasks of a highly complex nature. One was to place a value on 453,000 separate parcels of land abandoned by refugees in their flight from Palestine in 1948. Some of these plots were owned jointly by more than one refugee. A second achievement of PCC was to obtain the release of some Arab bank accounts in Palestine, initially blocked after the 1948 war. The Israeli government, through the medium of PCC, also authorized the release of refugee-owned contents of a number of safe deposit boxes in Israeli banks.

In ways not central to the Palestine dispute, United Nations agencies operate in the Middle East, as they do in other underdeveloped parts of the world. At least 11 Middle Eastern countries have received technical assistance from the United Nations Technical Assistance Board (TAB), the United Nations International Children's Emergency Fund (UNICEF), and UNESCO. Activities of these agencies impinge on the Arab-Israeli conflict, when they minister in various ways to the refugee population.

Israeli Attitude Toward United Nations

Over the years many Israelis have become increasingly disillusioned with the United Nations because of a voting pattern that has developed within the world body. Beginning in the mid-1950s, when the Israeli army began mounting reprisal raids against Jordan, Syria, and Egypt, the United Nations frequently voted censure of the Jewish state. Impelling this condemnation was the fact that Israeli armed forces, while executing reprisal raids, often killed Arab civilians, regardless of age or sex. In the first such reprisal raid by Israel, against the Jordanian village of Qibya on October 14, 1953, a battalion of the Israeli army surrounded the village at night, dynamited its buildings, and killed more than 50 Arab men, women, and children.

To Israelis the pattern of U.N. condemnations was unfair, because the censure votes seemed to them to ignore the fact that Arab incursions over periods of weeks and months had caused at least as much damage as the one-shot Jewish reprisal raids. A recent example was a Security Council resolution of March 26, 1969, condemning Israel for its air force attack near the Jordanian town of Salt. Israel claimed the raid had knocked out an Arab terrorist base. The Jordan government said only civilian targets had been hit, including a rest house for travelers.

Israelis accused the Security Council six of whose members at that time refused to have diplomatic relations with the Jewish state—of applying a double standard. Arab terrorists could act with impunity, while Israel was censured for trying to destroy the centers from which the guerrillas attacked. Jewish officials argued that only once in 20 years had the Security Council passed a resolution favoring Israel. That was 18 years ago, when the Council upheld Israel's right to use the Suez Canal.[2] On other occasions, however, Israeli diplomatic efforts succeeded in preventing votes adverse to the Jewish state or in persuading major powers to abstain on key issues.

The United Nations' Latest Word

The United Nations' most recent definitive word on the Palestine problem is the Security Council resolution of November 22, 1967. The language of its various points suggests how little down the road toward peace Arabs and Israelis have moved in the past two decades, since the United Nations first grappled with the conflict. The resolution stated:

> The Security Council,
> Expressing its continuing concern with the grave situation in the Middle East,

---

[2] Francis Ofner, *The Christian Science Monitor,* April 3, 1969.

Emphasizing the inadmissibility of the acquisition of territory by war and the need to work for a just and lasting peace in which every State in the area can live in security,

Emphasizing further that all Member States in their acceptance of the Charter of the United Nations have undertaken a commitment to act in accordance with Article 2 of the Charter,

1. Affirms that the fulfillment of Charter principles requires the establishment of a just and lasting peace in the Middle East which should include the application of both the following principles:

(i) Withdrawal of Israeli armed forces from territories occupied in the recent conflict;

(ii) Termination of all claims or states of belligerency and respect for and acknowledgement of the sovereignty, territorial integrity and political independence of every State in the area and their right to live in peace within secure and recognized boundaries free from threats or acts of force;

2. Affirms further the necessity:

(i) For guaranteeing freedom of navigation through international waterways in the area;

(ii) For guaranteeing the territorial inviolability and political independence of every State in the area, through measures including the establishment of demilitarized zones;

3. Requests the Secretary-General to designate a Special Representative to proceed to the Middle East to establish and maintain contacts with the States concerned in order to promote agreement and assist efforts to achieve a peaceful and accepted settlement in accordance with the provisions and principles in this resolution;

4. Requests the Secretary-General to report to the Security Council on the progress of the efforts of the Special Representative as soon as possible.

Chosen by Secretary General U Thant as his special representative was, as we have seen, Swedish diplomat Gunnar Jarring. "For its part," declared President Johnson on September 10, 1968, "the United States of America has fully supported the efforts of . . . Ambassador Jarring, and we shall continue to do so."

Mr. Johnson also spotlighted Jerusalem as "a critical issue" in any peace settlement. "No one wishes," the President said, "to see the Holy City again divided by barbed wire and by machineguns. I therefore . . . urge an appeal to the parties to stretch their imaginations so that their interests and all the world's interests in Jerusalem, can be taken fully into account in any final settlement." This was less explicit than a United Nations General Assembly resolution, passed almost unanimously, which condemned Israel's annexation of the Old City of Jerusalem after the 1967 war. The United States abstained on the vote.

Among the major parties directly involved, the United Nations resolution of November 22, 1967 has been accepted as a basis from which to work by Israel, Egypt, and Jordan, but rejected by Syria and Iraq. Even among the powers accepting the resolution, there is wide divergence on the issues involved—on the future of Jerusalem, for example, and on where Arab-Israeli frontiers finally should be drawn.

VIII. ISRAEL'S INTERNAL STRUCTURE

What is a Jew? The Israeli's answer was precise. "Anyone born of a Jewish mother is a Jew," he replied. "Traditionally we don't inquire about the father."

Must the mother be religious? "Not at all," answered the Israeli. Many Israelis, he acknowledged, wanted to belong to the Jewish nation, but not to the Jewish religion.

I recalled a distinguished Jewish woman, member of a kibbutz, who had gone to the United States on an Israeli bond drive. As the guest of a wealthy Jewish family in Boston, she had been invited to attend the local synagogue on Saturday. The visitor had declined, explaining that she was not religious. Her hostess had been shocked. A citizen of Israel, raising money for her country, and not religious!

"What is your religion?" the guest had then asked tartly. "To live here in comfort, sprinkle salt on your food, and pray 'next year in Jerusalem'? I have *gone* to Jerusalem, and worked as a pioneer on the land! That is my religion." [1]

Judaism as a creed had lost its hold on this woman. Yet her sense of Jewishness —of the separate identity of her people—was as strong as ever. Indeed, it had driven her to leave Europe and to work in Palestine under pioneering conditions that would have been rejected as too demanding by many religious Jews.

Loopholes exist in the traditional definition of a Jew, as a recent disagreement between the Israeli Supreme Court and the Knesset showed. An officer of the Israeli navy, Lt. Cmdr. Benyamin Shalit, had wanted his children to be registered as belonging to the Jewish nation, but not to Judaism as a religion. The government refused his petition, on the grounds that his wife—an English Christian woman— was not a Jew. She could have become Jewish by adopting the religion. But this Mrs. Shalit refused to do, because she was an atheist.

---

[1] Ellis, *Israel and the Middle East, op. cit.*, p. 41.

The commander took his case to the Supreme Court, which, on January 23, 1970, broke historic ground by ruling that the child of a Jewish father and a non-Jewish mother was still a Jew. The court, by a 5-4 vote, ordered the government to register the Shalit children as Jewish. The court's ruling appeared to mean that any person with at least one Jewish parent had the right to belong to "Le'um Hayehudi," or "the Jewish people wherever they are."

Chief Rabbi Yitzhak Nissim led the fight of religious Jews to overturn the court's ruling. "The Jewish people's nationhood," declared the chief rabbi, "is its religion and its religion is its nationality." The problem facing Golda Meir's coalition government was political, for the National Religious Party, headed by Interior Minister Moshe Shapiro, threatened to quit the coalition, if the court decision were not reversed.

Finally a majority of the cabinet agreed on two key amendments to Israel's Law of Return. A person would be registered as a Jew only if his mother was Jewish and he had not embraced another religion. A person also could gain Jewish nationality by converting to Judaism. The second amendment required that non-Jewish husbands and wives, and children of mixed marriages, should have the same rights as immigrating Jews.

The Knesset approved the two amendments and thus wrote into civil law for the first time the rabbinical definition of who is a Jew. This nullified the Supreme Court's ruling, but by no means settled the issue for large segments of the Israeli public. Demonstrations organized by the socialist Mapam party—also a member of the government coalition—protested the Knesset-approved amendments. Placards carried by demonstrators, many of them young people, read "Democracy, not Theocracy," "Separate state from religion," and "We are Jews of the twentieth century and not of the Egyptian Exodus."

The contretemps arising from Commander Shalit's case appeared to leave the matter as follows. A non-Jew could become a citizen of Israel, as before. But the rabbinate, by law now and not only by custom, would decide on the Jewishness of an individual, based on the mother's status. A nonbeliever who was born of a Jewish mother—who also might not be religious—still was classified as a Jew by the rabbinical definition. But an outsider—that is, any person born of a non-Jewish mother—could become Jewish only by embracing Judaism.

The above discussion applies particularly to citizens of Israel. But what about Jews who have no intention of living in the Zionist state? They may have no common language (unless Hebrew secondarily) and little shared cultural background. A Soviet Jew, for example, differs greatly in outlook and aspirations from a Jewish citizen of the United States or of Argentina. Scholars find no easy way to define Jewishness today, since the secular revolution robbed Jewishness of its central religious connotation.

"The truth is," writes Jacob Neusner, "today there is no such thing as a single Jewish identity, as there assuredly was in times past an identity one could define in meaningful terms. Jewishness now is a function of various social and cultural settings, and is meaningful in those settings only." [2]

---

[2] Jacob Neusner, "Zionism and The Jewish Problem," *Midstream,* November 1969.

86

There is no single "Jewish way" of organizing experience, Neusner continues, nor a universally shared concept of Jewish history. The State of Israel provides a rallying point for those Jews who live in Palestine. But for outsiders, enmeshed in disparate national, religious, and secular identities, the definition of Jewishness becomes a problem for individual conscience and decision.

Church and State in Israel

Judaism is not the state religion of Israel, in the sense that Islam is of Syria or Roman Catholicism is of Spain. Neither, however, is there complete separation of church and state as in the United States. Israel's Proclamation of Independence guaranteed equal rights to all religious communities. The government, the proclamation said, "will safeguard the Holy Places of all religions."

Apart from the normal legal structure—magistrates' courts, district courts, and Supreme Court—special religious courts exist in Israel. Each major community has its own religious courts of first instance and appeal, which rule on matters of personal status according to the applicable religious law—Rabbinical (Jewish), Shari'a (Moslem), Druze, or various Christian codes. Moslem courts have complete jurisdiction over their members in all matters of personal status. Jewish and Christian courts rule in matters of marriage, divorce, alimony, and some other aspects of personal status. Israelis of whatever faith go to a religious court to obtain a divorce. Americans of whatever faith, by contrast, apply to civil courts.

Israeli civil law requires a religious marriage ceremony, which may be Jewish, Moslem, Druze, or Christian as the case may be.

A Ministry of Religious Affairs cooperates with leaders of the various religious communities, as does the Department of Antiquities and Museums in restoring hallowed sites. Each community has the right to enjoy its own weekly day of rest— Friday for Moslems, Sunday for Christians—and to celebrate its holy days.

But here strict equality ends, for the vast majority of Israeli citizens are Jewish. Thus the nation's official weekly holiday is Saturday, the Jewish Sabbath. On this day no buses or other public transportation are supposed to run. "Yet," remarked one Israeli, "the municipality of Haifa decided differently and Haifa buses run on Saturday."

All Israeli citizens, whether Jewish, Christian, or Moslem, eat kosher food when they fly El Al or when they dine in a restaurant belonging to the government. Jewish dietary laws are observed in the Israeli armed forces and in public institutions. Jewish children study Bible and Talmud as part of their regular school education. In such matters rabbinical authority impinges on what most Americans would consider to be the prerogatives of the state.

"What we have in Israel," explained a senior government official, "is a compromise in the area of church and state. This suits the needs of the great majority of our citizens." There were, however, extremist Jews who wanted "either a complete theocracy or a completely atheistic state."

At one extreme was Naturei Karta, a miniscule group of perhaps 200 families who rejected any form of registration, refused to pay taxes, and declined to recognize the State of Israel. Adherents of Naturei Karta were anti-Zionist, holding that establishment of the State of Israel must await the coming of the Messiah. Allied to this group but politically weightier was Agudat Israel, an ultra-Orthodox religious community. Members of Agudat Israel accepted the legitimacy of the state, but favored a theocracy under rabbinical control.

"Then," continued the Israeli, "we have the National Religious Party, made up of people who want rabbinical law to have greater influence in shaping the secular law of the state. They do not demand a complete theocracy, but stand for what might be called religious Zionism." This bloc had been formed in 1956 by the union of Mizrahi and its labor wing, Hapoel Hamizrahi.

At the other end of the scale were atheist Jews, who wanted total separation of church and state. "In between," concluded the Israeli, "is the great mass of citizens, who generally agree that religious strife must be avoided and who therefore accept the present system."

A Jew, whether atheist or religious, shares in all rights and privileges accorded by the Jewish state. But for non-Jews there has been in practice discrmination running deeper than the necessity to eat kosher food in government restaurants or to conform to rabbinical transportation laws. The Proclamation of Independence referred to ancient Hebrew prophets who must be upheld. This in itself foreshadowed less than complete equality for non-Jewish Israelis. Arab-Jewish tension led to the banning of Israeli Arabs, except Druze citizens, from the armed forces.

Non-Jews cannot aspire to the highest positions in government. In this sense Israel appears to be less tolerant than Egypt, which permits Coptic Christians in the cabinet and, of course, Lebanon, whose government is based on a careful sharing of responsibility among the religious communities.

Oriental Versus European Jews

During the mandate days, Jewish immigration to Palestine was overwhelmingly European in origin. From 1919 until May 1948, when the State of Israel was founded, 89.6 percent of all Jewish immigrants came from America, Europe, and Oceania. Only 10.4 percent of Jewish immigrants came from Africa and Asia.

After the first Arab-Jewish war the scales tipped the other way and, between 1948 and today, Israel took in more than half a million "oriental" Jews from Arab lands—Morocco, Algeria, Egypt, Iraq, and others. During the period 1948-66 nearly 55 percent of all Jewish immigrants were from Asia and Africa.

Oriental Jews already may number more than half the total population of Israel. "In any event," admitted an Israeli, "we are approaching that point, not only because of immigration, but because Asian and African Jews have a higher birth rate than those from Europe." This situation created social tension in the Jewish state and foreboding for the future among many Israelis of European origin.

"I would not compare it to the Negro-white conflict in the United States," declared an Israeli official, "not at all. Ours is the sociological problem of people who have come from entirely different cultural backgrounds. All Jews in Israel have the same *rights,*" he insisted, "but not the same *possibilities.*"

He likened it to the situation in Britain, where, he commented, "if someone comes from the lower social strata, he must have great talent to break through.

The problem is more complicated in Israel, because our people came from different countries."

On one point he was emphatic. There was no political alliance or any other common interest between Israeli Arabs and Israeli oriental Jews, the two less privileged classes of the country. "If there are any Jews who hate the Arabs," the official confided, "it is those who have come to Israel from Arab lands."

The great concern of European Israelis is to prevent what one described as the "Levantinization" of their nation. "We want to lift the Asian and African Jews to European standards," he stressed, "not lower our standards to theirs." If the latter happened, Israel would become what European Zionists never had conceived or wanted—one oriental country living among others in the Middle East.

"We cannot solve our integration problem in one generation," acknowledged an Israeli official, "but we are on the way to solving it." Sabras—Jews born in Palestine—were beginning to share a common point of view, regardless of family origin. This was especially true within kibbutzim, the official added. In cities, he conceded, a kind of ghetto system still prevailed, with oriental Jews clustering to themselves.

An Israeli from Europe and I were strolling down a main street of Tel Aviv, when a group of dark-complexioned people passed us. Were they Jews or Arabs? I asked. "I don't know," he confessed, staring after them. "I can't tell unless there is something about their clothing that gives them away."

Army as Integration Force

The Israeli army is the nation's prime instrument of social integration. At the age of 18 every Israeli youth is inducted for 36 months of active service, after which he passes into the reserves. Unmarried Israeli women must serve for 20 months, unless exempted on religious grounds. Those exempted are assigned to teaching or social work for their period of service. Should a woman marry while on active duty, she is transferred automatically to the reserves. As soon as she has children she is excused from all military service.

Druze and Circassian youth serve in the Israeli defense forces. But Israel's Arab citizens, other than Druze, are excluded from military service. Officials fear that Arabs in uniform might act as a fifth column, passing military intelligence to the enemy. This poses a dilemma for Israeli policymakers, who strive to convince the nation's 390,000 Arabs that they are not second-class citizens. This claim is belied by the government's evident doubt that Arab men in uniform would be loyal to the Jewish state.

Since many recruits are bewildered newcomers to Palestine, the army tries to give each soldier a sense of belonging to Israel. Oriental Jews often are illiterate in Hebrew, Israel's national language. During their first six months such recruits receive 180 hours of Hebrew instruction and this teaching is carried on throughout their period of military service. Recruits illiterate in any language—about 3 to 4 percent of the total—go first to a three-week school on Mount Carmel, near Haifa. When they complete this school, they begin their formal military training.

Once the language barrier has been removed, army lessons include a history of the Jewish people from ancient times to the present. Contributions made by each national group to world Jewry are stressed. Jews from Spain or Iraq, for example, learn that at periods during Jewish history their communities shone as cultural centers of the Diaspora. These lessons are supplemented by field trips throughout Israel, to study the geography of the country and to inspect sites famous in Jewish history.

Teams of performers—singers, musicians, actors, all serving in the army—travel from unit to unit, teaching soliders the songs and dances of their new land. Such artists, instead of serving a month of ordinary active duty during their reserve years, give a certain number of performances before army groups.

A lieutenant must pass a teaching course to be promoted to captain. Captains and majors study the development of Israel as an expression of Jewish life. Lieutenant colonels and colonels take a course in ancient Hebrew literature, based on the Bible and Talmud. A series of booklets describes the histories of Jewish communities throughout the world—Russian, American, Yemeni, Iraqi, and so on.

Soldiers are taught to regard the Arabs as temporary enemies, but as people with whom Israel aspires to live in peace. Knowledge of Arab history and the Arab way of life is imparted to recruits.

Finally, there is Nahal (Pioneer Fighting Youth). After intensive military training, including commando techniques, Nahal groups of young people are assigned to kibbutzim to learn farming. Then they found new villages in isolated or dangerous parts of the country. Kibbutzim springing up on the Golan Heights were founded by Nahal.

This variegated army education is a supplement to formal military training. Object of the whole program is to return to civilian life not only experienced soldiers, available for rapid call-up in times of stress, but men and women who feel themselves part of Israel, whatever their cultural or national origins may have been.

Israel's defense forces are made up of three components—a small nucleus of professional officers and noncoms, a draft contingent undergoing training, and a large body of reserves. These reserves, capable of being mobilized within 48 hours, formed the bulk of Israel's victorious army in 1967. Men remain in the reserves until the age of 49, undergoing a month's training yearly until they are 40, and 14 days annually thereafter. Unmarried women remain reservists until the age of 34.

The professional cadre of the armed forces totals 22,500 officers and men. This can be raised to approximately 290,000 by mobilization of reserves. Of this total the army has 11,500 regulars and 268,000 at full strength. The navy has 3,000 cadre and 7,000 men when fully mobilized. The air force contains 8,000 regulars, plus 7,000 reservists.[3]

Immigration and Emigration

The early waves of Jewish immigration to Palestine, called Aliyas and stretching from 1882-1924, have been described, as has the flood of newcomers during the mandate period and the early years of statehood. Immigration figures for each year of statehood to the present are as follows:

---

[3] *The Military Balance 1969-1970* (London: The Institute for Strategic Studies, 1969).

1948	101,828
1949	239,576
1950	170,249
1951	175,095
1952	24,369
1953	11,326
1954	18,370
1955	37,478
1956	56,234
1957	71,224
1958	27,082
1959	23,895
1960	24,510
1961	47,638
1962	61,328
1963	64,364
1964	54,716
1965	30,736
1966	15,730
1967	14,327
1968	30,000
1969	39,000
Total:	1,339,073[4]

There are still many more Jews outside Israel than in the country. Broadly speaking, the remaining Diaspora falls into two categories—those who would go to Israel (or somewhere else) if they could and those who are content to stay where they are. The nearly six million American Jews—2,380,000 of whom live in New York City alone—are the prime example of the latter. No bars keep American Jewish citizens from emigrating. Some, indeed, have gone to Israel. I met a chaver in a kibbutz near Gaza who insisted that, from the time she was a little girl in New York, she had attended Zionist camps in the United States and had been taught that her goal in life was to go to Israel. She was deeply satisfied with her kibbutz career in Palestine. But the vast majority of American Jews prefer to remain in the United States.

Second largest community of the Diaspora lives in the Soviet Union. Soviet Jews number 2,485,000, of whom 400,000 live in Moscow and 170,000 in Odessa.[5] No one can be sure how many Soviet Jews would leave, and to what new homelands they would go, if emigration restrictions were to be lifted by the Kremlin. But the assumption is that many thousands of newcomers might flock to Israel.

---

[4] Israeli government figures, except for the year 1969. Unofficial immigration figures for this year were supplied by the Jewish Agency for Israel in Frankfurt, West Germany.

[5] Diaspora figures in this section were supplied by the Israeli government. Independent sources differed by a few thousands, in some cases more, in others less. But substantially the sources agreed with Israeli official estimates.

Some Jews in Communist lands say they want to go to Israel and then choose other destinations. This was particularly true of Polish Jews, during the recent period of relative freedom to emigrate. Jews leaving the country had to surrender their passports to Polish officials, who accompanied them on trains to Vienna. In Vienna the Polish authorities handed the passports to the various Jewish agencies which had contracted to forward the emigrés to Israel.

Once out of the clutches of Polish authority, those Jews who wanted to live in Europe or the United States were powerless to get their travel papers back from the Jewish agencies. The latter did not object to the emigrés' choice of homeland. But if the agencies were to connive with Jews to get out of Poland, ostensibly to go to Israel, and then allow them to travel elsewhere, the whole arrangement might have collapsed.

I met a Jewish couple who had traveled the Warsaw-Vienna route and then clandestinely, without papers, had made their way to West Germany, where they wanted to live. Once inside the Federal Republic they had had no problem, for, by reason of ancestry, they qualified as ethnic Germans under German law. Both husband and wife had spent months in Nazi concentration camps in Poland. Yet two decades later they chose the Federal Republic over Israel as a place to live, because, the husband said, "they would be more at home there." He did not say so, but the couple also was eligible for West German government compensation given to refugees from the east.

Many Tunisian Jews, reared on French culture, chose France as a place to live, rather than Israel. This also was true of some Jews from Algeria and Morocco. Not all Jews, in other words, looked upon Israel as their particular promised land.

Following is a breakdown of Diaspora communities, except for the United States and the Soviet Union, which already have been described. The first list includes countries from which Jews generally would be free to emigrate if they chose.

France	520,000 Jews
Great Britain	450,000
Turkey	45,000
Belgium	40,000
Italy	35,000
West Germany	32,000
Holland	23,000
Switzerland	20,000
Sweden	13,000
Austria	11,000
Denmark	9,000
Greece	6,500
Spain	5,000
Finland	1,500
Luxembourg	900
Norway	800

Also in this category are Latin American countries, whose Jewish communities number as follows.

Argentina	400,000
Uruguay	45,000
Chile	30,000
Mexico	25,000
Colombia	10,000
Venezuela	8,000
Bolivia	4,000
Peru	3,500
Ecuador	2,000
Brazil	1,200

Next come Communist nations, whose rules on Jewish emigration vary, but generally are restrictive.

Romania	120,000
Hungary	80,000
Poland	22,000
Czechoslovakia	16,000
Yugoslavia	7,500
Bulgaria	7,000
East Germany	3,000
Albania	300

Exact figures on the numbers of Jews in some Communist lands are difficult to obtain. The case of Poland has been cited, where clandestinely-allowed emigration is not reflected in latest statistics released by Polish authorities. East Germany, too, is estimated by some expert sources to have no more than 1,500 Jews, though published figures still speak of 3,000.

Finally, a substantial number of Jews remain in Arab lands. The 50,000 figure for Morocco indicates the reluctance of Moroccan authorities to allow their Jews to leave.

Morocco	50,000
Tunisia	20,000
Libya	5,000
Lebanon	5,000
Syria	4,000
Iraq	3,400
Algeria	2,500
Yemen	2,000
Egypt	1,800

One hears a good deal about the number of Jews who go to Israel. Less is heard about those Israelis who, for a variety of reasons, pull up stakes and leave the Zionist state. There were times during the British mandate, particularly during the 1926-28 depression years, when more Jews left Palestine than came in. In

1927, according to British authorities, the net loss of Jews to the Yishuv was more than 2,000. The next year the net immigration to Palestine was ten persons.

Movement out of the country continued after statehood. The following figures show total emigration from Israel during the first nine years of the country's existence. A minute fraction of those who left were non-Jewish.

1948	almost no emigration
1949	almost no emigration
1950	9,966
1951	10,476
1952	13,500
1953	13,000
1954	7,500
1955	6,400
1956	8,000

The Israeli government is reluctant to disclose exact emigration figures for recent years. They concede there have been three waves of emigration since the state was founded. The first was the 1951-53 period, as the above figures show. The excess of emigrants over immigrants in 1953 was nearly 2,000. The second emigration wave, according to Israeli officials, was in 1956 and the last took place in 1965. Economic reasons apparently impelled most emigrants to leave. Domestic price increases of more than 50 percent in the 1960-66 period helped to trigger the most recent outflow. Most emigrés, Israeli sources said, went to the United States and Canada, with some choosing Western European countries.

"Security reasons were not involved," one official commented. "Since the 1967 war emigration has about dried up. In fact, some people who had left came back to Israel, when they knew the country was in danger."

To many Zionists, it is hard to admit that substantial numbers of Jews prefer to live outside Israel and that some Israelis, having tasted life in the Promised Land, choose to leave. Sensitivity on this point explains why emigration figures—unlike those for immigration—are omitted from government publications.

IX. WHERE THE POWER IS

One writes about Israel's political parties today in a different context than before the 1967 war, for opinion on the state's crucial dilemma—what to do with the occupied territories and their nearly one million Arabs—cuts across party lines. Some leaders in almost all parties advocate withdrawal after a peace settlement, others argue for holding on. This is a national problem, transcending party discipline.

Within the Israel Labor party, for example, nationally-known figures disagree on the future of occupied lands. Pinhas Sapir, secretary-general of the party, and Foreign Minister Abba Eban are against permanent retention. Mr. Eban weighs the adverse effect on world opinion of such a policy. Mr. Sapir harks back to the Zionist goal of creating a Jewish state, using Jewish labor. To integrate the new lands and their Arabs, he believes, would create a Jewish superstructure, based on Arab labor. This would contravene Zionism and the meaning of the state.

Defense Minister Moshe Dayan, also within the Israel Labor party, claims that, so long as Israel occupies the Arab lands, the government has a duty toward their people. The state should give Arabs living under Israeli rule the maximum access possible to government aid. This should include job opportunities within Israel. At present an estimated 10,000-15,000 Arabs of the West Bank and Gaza have found work in Israel. General Dayan favors this, as creating a common interest between Arabs and Jews.

Deputy Prime Minister Yigal Allon urges the establishment of agricultural and urban settlements along the eastern fringes of the West Bank. He does not prejudge the ultimate disposition of the area, but believes the existence of Jewish settlements would provide a secure frontier into the future. These disparate views, all grouped beneath the umbrealla of the Israel Labor party, illustrate the difficulty of categorizing party views on Israel's basic dilemma.

Political Spectrum, from Left to Right

In 1965 the *Communist Party of Israel* split into two rival parties—Rakah (Reshima Kommunistit Hadasha) and Maki (Miflaqe Kommunistit Yisre'elit).

Maki, with one deputy in the 120-member Knesset, supported Israeli policy during the 1967 war and wants no withdrawal from the occupied territories before a peace settlement with the Arabs. Leaders of Maki include Dr. Moshe Sneh, who headed the Haganah defense force until 1946, and Shmuel Mikunis, Maki's Knesset member.

Rakah, with three Knesset seats, toes the Moscow line and demands Israeli withdrawal from occupied lands. Two of Rakah's three deputies—Tewfik Toubi and Emil Habibi—are Arab, reflecting the fact that this party derives much support from Israel's Arab citizens, who see within Rakah an opportunity to demonstrate legally against the state. Jewish Communists, by contrast, tend to stick with Maki.

The Knesset is elected by proportional representation, so the ratio of three seats to one indicates that Rakah is three times as large as Maki. Both parties stand for a Marxist-Leninist approach to economic and social problems.

Mapam (Mifleget Hapo'alim Hameuhedet, or United Workers' party), submitted a joint list of candidates with the Israel Labor party during national elections October 28, 1969. Mapam hews to classical Marxist ideology, but within a democratic framework. Hence Mapam stands to the left of Social Democratic parties in Europe.

Before independence Mapam argued for a bi-national Arab-Jewish state in Palestine and later the party worked hard to eliminate discrimination against Israel's Arab citizens. The party was instrumental in having the laws abolished which for years kept many Israeli Arabs under military surveillance. Mapam, faithful to its concept of a bi-national state, welcomes Arab members. Mapam leaders include Victor Schemtov and Israel Barzilai, both ministers without portfolio.

Next on the political spectrum comes Israel's most important grouping, the *Israel Labor Party* (Mifleget Ha'avoda Hayisre'elit). This was founded in 1968 by the fusion of Mapai, Achdut Ha'avoda-Poalei Zion, and Rafi. With its affiliated Arab lists, and including Mapam seats, the Israel Labor party boasts 56 Knesset seats and has 12 Cabinet ministers, including Prime Minister Golda Meir, Deputy Premier Yigal Allon, Defense Minister Moshe Dayan, Foreign Minister Abba Eban, and Finance Minister Pinhas Sapir.

Broadly speaking, the Israel Labor party resembles European Social Democratic parties in economic policy. The party is socialist, but supports the continued existence of free enterprise and cooperative sectors of the economy. As we have seen, the party expresses conflicting views on the future of the occupied Arab lands.

Key leaders of Rafi include General Dayan and Shimon Peres, minister of immigration. Originally Rafi was formed by the breakaway from Mapai of former Prime Minister David Ben-Gurion and his followers. When the Israel Labor party was founded in January 1968, Ben-Gurion refused to join the merger and sat in the Knesset as an independent until his retirement.

Strongman of the Achdut branch of the Israel Labor party is Yigal Allon. Other important members are Minister without Portfolio Israel Galili and Moshe Carmel. Golda Meir and Abba Eban represent the old Mapai, as does the influential Pinhas Sapir, finance minister and secretary-general of the Israel Labor party.

A number of political groups use the word liberal to define their parties. In 1961 the Liberal party was formed by the merger of the General Zionists and Progressives, a collection of businessmen and intellectuals who favored free enterprise. Members of the old General Zionist and Progressive parties had come generally from Germany and other parts of Western Europe.

In 1965 the Liberal party formed an alliance with Herut, called *Gahal* (Gush Herut-Liberaliim) or the *Herut-Liberal Bloc*. This bloc, which believes in free enterprise, submits joint lists of candidates for elections and also works as a unit within the Knesset and the Histadrut. Gahal holds 26 Knesset seats.

Herut (Freedom), at the far right of the Israeli political spectrum, was founded in 1948 by Menahem Begin, leader of the Irgun Zvai Leumi terrorist organization. Herut always has been expansionist, advocating the territorial integrity of Israel within its historical Biblical boundaries. "More or less," declared one knowledgeable observer, "this means that Herut wants Israel to hold the conquered lands. But Herut never wanted an Israel from the Nile to the Euphrates, as some people have charged.

"In fact," he continued, "the Sinai did not really interest Herut. Its main thrust was to the east, to the other side of the Jordan River. Begin and his party still want the Jewish state to expand beyond the Jordan."

Begin was a Polish Jew who became the most notorious Jewish terrorist leader in Palestine during the mandate. "In my youth," confessed one Israeli, "I loathed Begin and considered him a typical Fascist demagogue. But I must admit that today he has mellowed, although his party still wants Israel to expand."

Ben-Gurion used to say he would form a government coalition with any party, except the Communists on the left and Herut on the right. But the pressures of national emergency brought Herut into the government for the first time, when a government of National Unity, led first by Levi Eshkol, was formed on June 5, 1967. That government, headed by Golda Meir, included the Israel Labor party, Mapam, the Herut-Liberal bloc, the National Religious party, and the Independent Liberal party. The Communists are excluded.

Until August 1970 Herut held three ministries. Then Mr. Begin withdrew his Herut colleagues from the government, in protest against Mrs. Meir's acceptance of the American proposed cease-fire plan. The three liberal ministers of the Gahal bloc also resigned.

When the main Liberal party merged with Herut, a small group of Liberals refused to go along. They called themselves the *Independent Liberal party* and today hold four Knesset seats and have one man, Minister of Tourism Moshe Kol, in the cabinet. Like the Herut-Liberal bloc, the Independent Liberals favor an economy based on free enterprise.

A small party called the *Free Center Movement* (Hamerkaz Hahofshi), with two Knesset seats, was founded in 1967, after splitting with Herut. The Free Center Movement wants Israel to retain the occupied Arab lands, favors free enterprise, and urges the government to assume control of health and social services. Currently these are administered by Histadrut, Israel's trade union organization.

We come now to Israel's three religious parties, already mentioned in the section on church and state. Foremost among these is the *National Religious Party* (Miflaqa Datit Leumit), founded in 1956 by a merger of Mizrahi and Hapoel Hamizrahi. This party, which favors legislation founded on the laws of the Torah, has 12 Knesset seats and two Cabinet ministers. One of these ministries concerns religious affairs. The other is the interior ministry. From the time the state was founded these "center religionists" have commanded about their present share of Knesset strength.

The National Religious party fought in vain to prevent Israeli television from broadcasting on Saturday. But, except in Haifa and Beersheba, the party has succeeded in banning public transport on the Sabbath.

Agudat Israel, with six seats, is in the opposition, though it was invited to join the government. This ultra-Orthodox group wants a complete theocracy, but does accept the authority of the government. Allied to Agudat Israel is *Poalei Agudat Israel,* a movement of religious workers, founded in 1924.

Completing the list of political parties is *Ha'olam Hazeh* (New Force), which stands for separation of church and state, neutrality in foreign relations, and cooperation between the Arab and Jewish national movements. Founded in 1965, Ha'olam Hazeh has two Knesset seats.

Also in the Knesset is a bloc of four deputies, headed by former Prime Minister David Ben-Gurion until his retirement. Finally, a "minorities" group commands four parliamentary seats.

Role of Knesset

Supreme legislative authority belongs to the Knesset, Israel's one-chamber parliament. Elected by universal suffrage for four years, this 120-seat body approves the cabinet and can dissolve a government by voting no confidence. Debates are conducted in Hebrew, but are translated simultaneously into Arabic for Arab deputies, who are allowed to speak in their own language. Laws passed by the Knesset cannot be invalidated by the Supreme Court.

As yet Israel possesses no constitution in the usual sense. In 1950 the Knesset resolved to enact from time to time fundamental laws. Taken together these eventually would form a constitution. One such bill was the "law of return," establishing the right of every Jew to immigrate to Israel. The Knesset elects the president of Israel for a term of five years. Since executive authority belongs to the cabinet and legislative power to the Knesset, the president's functions are largely ceremonial. He receives foreign ambassadors, signs laws and treaties after ratification, and —when a new government is to be formed—consults the parties and formally asks the appropriate party leader to select a cabinet.

Israel's electoral system of nationwide proportional representation is currently under challenge. Voters do not cast their ballots for individuals, but for lists presented by each party. The 120 Knesset seats then are sliced up like a pie among the parties, according to their percentage of the vote. If the Israel Labor party gets 35 percent of the vote, it receives 35 percent of Knesset seats and so on down the line. This means that voters often are not directly represented by deputies from their own districts.

98

Dov Joseph, a former minister of justice, observed recently that 300,000 residents of newly-settled areas had no representative in the Knesset, nor did the largely Arab area of Galilee. "The present system," Mr. Joseph said, "leaves no room for the electors to have influence over those who will represent them in the Knesset. They do not even know most of the candidates." [1]

A committee headed by Mr. Joseph recommends the formation of 30 new constituencies, each electing three deputies. This would create a link between voter and representative. Another 30 deputies would be separately elected on a list basis. If adopted, this system would combine proportional representation with constituency voting.

Other Sources of Power

"Power in Israel definitely does not lie with the army," remarked a senior Israeli official. "It should be a platitude to say this about a democratic nation, but the Israeli Army has played such a strategic role in preserving the state that people outside might regard it as a source of political power. It is not."

The professional army, he pointed out, was small. Citizen soldiers made up the bulk of the armed forces and they expressed themselves politically through their trade unions and parties, not through the army. An officer running for the Knesset had to resign his commission 100 days before the election.

Nor did power lie with the synagogue, the official added. It could not, in a country where perhaps 70 percent of the population was more or less non-observant religiously. Indirectly the rabbinate's view was conveyed through religious parties, operating in the political arena. But these parties played a minority role.

Doubtless the most powerful single organization in Israel is Histadrut, or the General Federation of Labor. This all-embracing trade union organization, to which more than one million Israelis belong, was founded in 1920, when there were about 5,000 Jewish workers in Palestine. These early settlers conceived of themselves as the pioneer force of a new nation which would be founded on the Zionist ideal of love of labor. To this end Histadrut became a national instrument for shaping workers' attitudes and, equally important, for creating sources of employment for newcomers.

This latter function launched Histadrut into the employment field. Today this labor federation is the nation's largest employer, owning enterprises of many kinds in virtually every branch of Israel's economy. In one way or another 90 percent of Israel's labor force is said to be connected with Histadrut.

The labor federation accepts as members academicians, doctors, lawyers, and other professionals, as well as the more ordinary class of worker. "We all belong to Histadrut," explained an Israeli diplomat, "for a simple reason. We want health and social insurance."

During the mandate period, when there was no Jewish government in Palestine, Histadrut organized health insurance and social benefits for workers of the Yishuv. This system carried on to the present day. Israel, often thought of as socialist-

---

[1] James Feron, *New York Times,* June 16, 1969.

oriented, has no comprehensive state-run social services, as do "capitalist" countries like West Germany and France. "We are a state with a social conscience," commented an Israeli, "but not yet a social welfare state, because of lack of money." As its circumstances permit the Israeli government bites deeper into the social welfare field. But the primary instrument in this area remains Histadrut. This dependence of almost all citizens on Histadrut protection keeps the labor federation's influence strong, quite apart from its ownership role in the economy.

To most Israelis there was nothing sinister about the growth of Histadrut. The labor federation was the only organization capable of training workers in new skills and at the same time opening job opportunities for workers to use their skills. Along the way Histadrut took on the task of supplying social services to its members.

More than 250,000 Israeli farmers in 550 kibbutzim and other types of villages belong to the Agricultural Workers' Union, connected with Histadrut. This organization deals with social, financial, and educational aspects of farm life. Tnuva, the agricultural marketing cooperative, handles over two-thirds of the nation's farm produce, including export sales. Another branch of Histadrut is the main supplier of goods to kibbutzim and cooperative villages. Nearly 100,000 young Israelis under 18 belong to Histadrut's organization of Working and Student Youth. Almost 500,000 women are members of the Women Workers' Council of Histadrut.

Among firms owned and operated by the labor federation are a building and public works company, an overseas and harbor works company, active in Africa and Asia, and an industrial holding company called Koor. Banks, ships, and newspapers are other properties belonging to Histadrut.

But the influence of the labor federation does not end with economics. Histadrut is organized politically, along party lines. This means, in effect, that the "same people who decide trade union policy also run the government," as one Israeli official put it. Many of the nation's top political leaders came from Histadrut ranks. The parties elect delegates to the Histadrut Convention, which selects a general council and an executive council. The latter in turn elects an executive bureau. Histadrut resembles a state within a state, whose political alignment closely reflects that of the nation at large.

Socialism requires careful definition, where Israel is concerned. Center of gravity of the nation's political life belongs to parties with a Marxist derivation. But most of these parties do not advocate nationalization of industry, nor does the state own much of the economy. Raw material industries, such as potash, phosphates, and copper, required state financing to launch them. Even in such industries, however, the tendency of the government is to relinquish its share to private control, where feasible.

"The greatest part of Israel's economy is in private hands," declared an official. But this, too, requires explanation. The largest "private" sector belongs in one way or another to Histadrut-affiliated organizations, primarily trade unions and cooperatives. This area of the economy outweighs the role played by private enterprise in the American sense. To this extent Israel is a socialist economy, but not in orthodox Marxist terms.

Essentials of the Economy

The economy with which both the Israeli government and Histadrut have grappled has run deeply in the red from 1948 to the present. The nation's population has trebled in the past two decades. This meant that economic production had to be trebled, simply to keep the standard of living from declining. In the early years of statehood, Israel's annual trade deficit ran between $250 and $300 million. In 1968, despite a sharp spurt of exports, the trade gap had grown to about $350 million and swelled further in 1969. In the first six months of 1970 the trade deficit rose 30 percent above the comparable period of 1969. On June 30 the 1970 trade deficit stood at $338 million.

Year by year this deficit has been covered by substantial outside contributions, of which the two most important—West German and United States aid, official and unofficial—have been detailed. Without these sources of income Israel scarcely could have survived, much less have progressed as an economic unit. When the Luxembourg aid agreement expired in 1966, one category of German assistance came to an end. This loss was made up by increased private donations from Western Jews, mainly American, after the six-day war. Israel's continuing problem is to cover of its balance-of-trade deficits with these outside contributions.

The government's annual budget, excluding defense, is divided into two parts—an ordinary budget and a development budget. The former is financed from local taxation. Income tax on individuals is levied progressively up to a maximum of 62.5 percent. A company pays 47.5 percent of its income in various taxes. The ordinary budget covers administrative expenses of the government, including the cost of social welfare and vocational training of newcomers.

The development budget goes toward expanding agriculture, industry, communications, and the construction of immigrant housing. A large part of this budget is financed from outside, through fund-raising drives of the United Jewish Appeal and the sale of State of Israel bonds. Foreign loans and U.S. government aid also go into the development budget.

Nearly one-third of Israel's total development costs are covered by revenue from State of Israel bonds. Five issues have been floated, beginning with the Independence Issue ($145 million) in May 1951. Next came the First Development Issue, worth $234 million, and a Second at $293 million. A Third Development Issue of $400 million was sold out during the crisis period of May-June 1967. A Fourth, worth $500 million, has been floated. These figures show that a constant factor in Israel's continued well-being remains the generosity of American Jews.

Money spent by American citizens to buy State of Israel bonds is not tax exempt in the United States. Donations to the United Jewish Appeal, however, are tax deductible to the donor, in the same way as contributions to American charities or religious organizations.

In ordinary years about 23 percent of the Israeli government budget—ordinary and development taken together—is spent on "economic purposes." These include subsidies to industry and farms, development of new lands and expansion of irrigation systems, the communications network, and the like.

Approximately 19 percent of the budget goes for social services—construction of new housing, development of the school system, and those sectors of social welfare which the government administers. Another 15 percent of the budget is consumed by debt repayments and other capital movements.

Next comes a category called "administration and security," totaling about 44 percent of the budget. The great bulk of this amount is allocated to defense. Visibly, the Israeli budget shows more than 40 percent of total expenditures going to defend the country.

The enourmous burden of defense spending—and Israel's continuing dependence on the generosity of American Jewry—were spotlighted by the 1970 budget, which Finance Minister Pinhas Sapir presented to the Knesset in February 1970. An unprecedented 25 percent of the nation's gross national product was to go for defense, including the purchase of military equipment abroad. Mr. Sapir, without disclosing details of the defense budget, said $1.2 billion—or 43 percent of the total $2.8 billion budget—would be devoted to security needs. This burden could only be borne, the finance minister made clear, if expected loans and gifts from abroad, principally from the American Jewish community, materialized.

Nondefense elements of the 1970 budget, which was 20 percent higher than that of the year before, also climbed sharply. Debt repayments were up 38 percent, while the ordinary and development budgets increased by 18 percent. Mr. Sapir explained to the Knesset that the budget was based on a taxation and wages policy which should allow the average Israeli to enjoy a 5 percent growth in his real income during 1970.

This policy in turn depended for success on the implementation of a two-year agreement signed February 1, 1970, by the government, industry, and Histadrut. This pact was designed to restrain wages, prices, and taxes for two years and thus, it was hoped, stave off devaluation of the Israeli pound. Wage increases gained by workers would be paid primarily in the form of government bonds, to avoid the inflationary effect of surplus capital competing on the market. Employers would match these "compulsory loans" of their workers by investing equal amounts in government bonds.

Growing domestic consumption was having the effect of widening the trade gap by boosting imports. This problem was compounded by the need to purchase expensive military hardware. As a result Israel, according to Mr. Sapir, was losing its foreign exchange reserves at the rate of $1 million a day early in 1970. Reserves at the end of 1969 stood at $328 million, down $281 million from the year before. Had wages been increased in the form of cash payments, Sapir stressed, excess purchasing power would have had to be soaked up in the form of higher taxes. The package deal achieved by government, manufacturers, and Histadrut—which, of course, sat on both employer and labor sides of the table in these negotiations—was aimed at preventing higher taxes by keeping prices in check.

Eminent Israeli economists, including David Horowitz, governor of the Bank of Israel and economics professors of the Hebrew University, criticized the "tripartite pact" as insufficient. Only devaluation and higher taxes, these experts claimed, could reduce the growing trade deficit.

The finance ministry predicted a deficit of $1.1 billion in the 1970 current account of the Israeli economy—that is, the excess of imports over exports of goods and services. The government was counting on loans and gifts from abroad to cover all but $100 million of this $1.1 billion deficit. Foreign capital imports, primarily from the American Jewish community and from restitutions paid by West Germany, had sufficed to balance the books each year through 1967. Then Israel had begun to dip into foreign exchange reserves to cover the deficit. Israel's holdings, which stood at $4.3 million in 1953, had climbed to $753 million at the end of 1967, before postwar demands started to drain them away.

Despite this dark picture, the Israeli economy has made substantial progress. In real terms the gross national product has grown 4.5 times since 1950, while the economy has expanded at an average annual rate of more than 9 percent. Production per capita has almost doubled since 1950, though many thousands of immigrant workers had to be trained almost from scratch upon arrival.

Structure of the economy resembles that of industrialized nations of Western Europe. Major segments of the domestic product include farming, 8.2 percent; industry, about 25 percent; private commerce and services, including tourism, 18.5 percent; government and public-sector expenditures, 19.5 percent, and construction, 6 percent. Defense expenses since the 1967 war have distorted this traditional breakdown by increasing the sector of government spending.

Since Israel is rich in skills and poor in natural resources, the nation's economy is oriented toward the export of finished products. Emphasis is placed on the export of diamonds, machinery, electrical and electronic components, fine chemicals, food products, and clothing.

The organizational framework of Israel's trade with West Germany illustrates the sophistication of the Jewish state's export drive. Three joint German-Israeli committees have been formed to market Israeli products in the Federal Republic. One handles textiles and fashions, a second works with metal products, and the third markets fruits and vegetables.

West German supermarket chains, on whose shelves tins of orange juice and other Israeli products already are familiar sights to German housewives, are members of the last-named committee. This group, headquartered in Frankfurt, plans to cut delivery time for Israeli foodstuffs from 12 to seven days where possible, by off-loading cargoes in southern European ports, like Trieste, and trans-shipping to West Germany by train.

Fresh flowers—roses, gladioli, iris, and others—are flown daily from Israel to West Germany. In 1968 West Germans bought Israeli flowers valued at $500,000.

Emphasis on finished manufactures of high quality and marketing committees established abroad in major customer countries are hallmarks of Israel's effort to become more nearly self-supporting. A major boost will come if and when Israel succeeds in signing an association agreement with the Common Market.

Economy of the Occupied Areas

Many concerned Israelis believe their government should do more to stimulate the Arab economies of the West Bank and Gaza. At present, according to a symposium held at the Hebrew University in Jerusalem June 12, 1969, economic output of the occupied areas totaled 500 million Israeli pounds yearly ($143 million), as against 14 billion pounds ($4 billion) for Israel itself.[2] A relatively modest investment of about $28 million would equal 20 percent of the gross national product of the occupied lands. Such an amount, prophesied Dr. Michel Bruno of Hebrew University, should not be hard for the Israeli government to attract from foreign agencies.

In addition, symposium members concluded, free trade and free movement of capital should be allowed between Israel and the Arab lands. Arab businessmen should be given tax incentives and loans to expand investment. Arab exports should be allowed to compete with Jewish goods on the Israeli market. Jewish businessmen should be encouraged to invest in the occupied lands, but not to build factories using Jewish management and Arab labor. This concept would contravene the Zionist ideal and would not develop Arab initiative.

Complications stand in the way of achieving the interchange advocated by the symposium Israeli price levels are much higher than those in Jordan. West Bank goods, particularly farm products, could undersell Israeli produce. Thus Arabs must get permits from the Israeli military government to market their goods in Israel. Authorities encourage West Bank residents to trade with Jordan or, alternatively, to export through outlets developed by Israel. The effect of all this is to insulate the Israeli economy from that of the West Bank and Gaza. Conversely, Arab merchants and farmers could not buy supplies from Jewish merchants at high Israeli prices.

Jordanian law still prevails in the West Bank. "No Israeli will invest his money in the West Bank under Jordanian law," declared an official. General Dayan urges the imposition of Israeli law on the occupied areas, as a stimulus to Israeli investment. Both currencies, Jordanian and Israeli, are legal tender in the West Bank.

In the early years of statehood zealous kibbutz experts longed to help Arab farmers in neighboring lands modernize their methods. Israelis wanted to expand their "Point Four" activities from Africa and Asia into Arab countries. Arab resistance was total. Now, however, Israelis are seizing a modest opportunity to teach West Bank farmers how to improve their crops. Already some Arab farmers in the occupied lands have switched to a brand of wheat suggested by Israeli specialists.

Israel derives certain benefits from the occupation, which help to offset administrative costs. Income from tourism in Jerusalem now goes entirely to the Jewish side. More important, Israel is pumping oil from former Egyptian fields in Sinai. This source of revenue and petroleum coincides with a dwindling of supplies from Israel's own small oil fields in the Negev.

---

[2] *The Jerusalem Post,* June 15, 1969.

104

X. CONCLUSION

When Israeli Foreign Minister Abba Eban visited West Germany in February 1970, more than 1,600 German policemen were detailed to guard his every move. In part the reason was to protect Mr. Eban against possible assault by Arab commandos, who—in the weeks before the Israeli visitor came—had been implicated in attacks on El Al passengers at Munich and on an Austrian Airlines plane at Frankfurt.

But left-wing German university students also had threatened to demonstrate against Mr. Eban, as the representative of a state which, in the students' eyes, practiced colonialism in occupied Arab lands. The attitude of these students had been forecast earlier at Munich, Frankfurt, and Hamburg, when leftist demonstrators had tried to shout Israeli Ambassador Asher Ben-Natan from university rostrums.

This form of anti-Israel protest was confined to the same small minority of students which periodically organizes street demonstrations against the West German university and social structures. In any event, the left-wing students failed to protest against Eban. But even their threat to do so, and their earlier hostility to the Israeli ambassador, would have been unthinkable in the German Federal Republic before the 1967 war.

The aftermath of that war—namely, the continued occupation by Israeli armed forces of Arab territories—evoked an image of colonialism in student thought. Not only in West Germany was this true. In Sweden also I found university students pamphleteering and lecturing against Israeli policy in the occupied lands.

For Israel the danger is that the longer the occupation goes on, accompanied by punitive strikes into Jordan and Egypt, and by the razing of Arab houses and other punishments in the administered zones, the less sympathy the Jewish state may find in the outside world. The fact that attacks by Arab terrorists against civil aircraft in European centers also shocks the world does not lessen the growing tendency to regard Israel as an occupying power.

To many persons, who have regarded the establishment of Israel primarily as an act of justice to a long-persecuted people, a deeper question may be raised. It was,

105

indeed, a humanitarian motive which impelled much support for the Zionist cause. But since the Zionist goal—establishment of a Jewish homeland in Palestine—displaced more than a million Arabs, and now leaves nearly a million more under military occupation, was not humanity toward the Jews accompanied by inhumanity toward the Arabs?

This problem belongs not alone to Israel, but affects directly United States policy and the American people. For, as has been seen, the continued progress of the Jewish state depends more and more on financial support from American Jews. The second largest form of capital import—restitution payments from West Germany—shrinks as individual Israeli recipients pass on. The burden of supporting Israel's burgeoning defense costs, as well as the development of its resources, falls heavily on the shoulders of American Jewish citizens. They, in turn, press the United States government to support the beleaguered Jewish state.

As a result, the United States is firmly anchored in Arab thought as the major friend of Israel. "The U.S.A. and its policy," declared President Nasser on February 2, 1970, "shoulders the greatest responsibility for what is going on in the Middle East and what will take place there in the future." America, the Egyptian leader continued, provided Israel with the "tools"—the weapons—with which "to perform its criminal role" against the Arabs.

The long-term results of the Arab-Israeli conflict on the American position in the Middle East are both strategic and economic. "One cannot compare," declared a key NATO defense minister privately, "Western security in the Mediterranean today with what it was when only the American Sixth Fleet cruised that sea." Now, the defense minister went on, a powerful Soviet fleet was stationed permanently in the Mediterranean, operating partly from Arab naval bases. The minister was not speaking in the context of the Arab-Israeli conflict. Nonetheless, it was the polarization of this conflict into Soviet support for the Arabs and American friendship for Israel which allowed Moscow to build a position of strength throughout much of the Middle East, including the presence of a Soviet fleet in the Mediterranean Sea.

As to economics, the chief American stake in the Middle East remains a continued flow of Arab oil to the Western world. The importance of access to Arab oil heightens as the Soviets near the point of becoming net importers of petroleum. In December 1969, a group of top American industrialists, with oil and other interests in the Middle East, was invited to confer with President Nixon in the White House. Reportedly the business leaders warned that America's political and economic influence with the Arabs was declining and that steps should be taken to improve United States relations with oil-producing Arab states and others.

On February 22, 1970, Libya's Premier Moamer Qadhafi declared at a press conference in Tripoli that his government would be willing to cut off Libya's oil shipments to the West, if asked to do so by President Nasser in the name of the Arab struggle against Israel. This might be regarded as an idle threat, since the premier would have the Libyan people to deal with, if overnight he eliminated their chief source of income. Nonetheless, countervailing signs lend possible weight to Qadhafi's words. Egyptian influence in Libya is growing. Cooperation among Egypt, Libya, and the Sudan is thickening. Some Arab sources speak of an eventual federation of the three North African lands, though Egyptian experience in its brief union with Syria, and Moslem-Negro strife in the Sudan, do not auger well for a federative success.

Meanwhile, the power bases of Washington's traditional friends in the Arab Middle East—King Hussein, the Saudi monarchy, and the Lebanese government—are eroding. This is especially true of King Hussein, who has been forced to make concessions to al-Fatah and to accept the guerrilla movement as virtually a state within a state in Jordan.

This study began with an analysis of the dilemma Israel faces—whether to remain an occupation power, or to give citizenship to one million additional Arabs and lose its identity as a Jewish state. A third alternative—backed by the United Nations and by the United States—the Israeli government refuses to contemplate, short of an overall peace agreement, negotiated directly with the Arabs. That alternative is a partial or complete withdrawal from Arab lands won in 1967.

Israel's dilemma, by extension, becomes that of the United States, chief supplier of military equipment and capital assistance to the Jewish state. Can the United States maintain its protective attitude toward Israel and still preserve essential American interests in the Arab world?

DATE DUE

MAY 26 '87			
MAY 1 4 '87			
MAR 3 1 '8?			
MAY 1 0 '89			
JUL 2 8 '89			
mending shelf 7-18-89			
GAYLORD			PRINTED IN U.S.A.